It's My Life
and I Live Here
One Woman's Story

Copyright © 2011, 2021 by Michelle Cameron

Published by Michelle G Cameron, LLC

Printed in the United States of America 2021— Second Edition

All rights reserved. Except as permitted under the U.S. Copyright Act of 1976, this publication shall not be broadcast, rewritten, distributed, or transmitted, electronically or copied, in any form, or stored in a database or retrieval system, without prior written permission from the author.

> Library of Congress Cataloging-in-Publications Data
> It's My Life and I Live Here - One Woman's Story/Michelle Cameron.
>
> ISBN 978-0-578-98674-6
>
> 1. Cameron, Michelle G. 2. Survival 3. Spiritual Growth 4. Personal Growth 5. Encouragement

Unless otherwise indicated, scripture quotations used and marked (NIV) are from the HOLY BIBLE, NEW INTERNATIONAL VERSION®, NIV® Copyright © 1973, 1978, 1984, 2011 by Biblica, Inc.™ Used by permission. All rights reserved worldwide.

Scripture quotations marked (KJV) are from the King James Version of the Bible. Copyright © All rights reserved.

Scripture quotations marked (NASB) are from taken from the NEW STANDARD BIBLE®. Copyright © 1960, 1962, 1963, 1968, 1971, 1972, 1973, 1975, 1977, 1995 by the Lockman Foundation. Used by permission.

Thank You!

Hello!

If this is your first time connecting with me or reading any of my books, welcome!

I want to extend a special Thank You for your support of my first edition of this book throughout the last ten years. I was nervous about releasing my personal, private story – but I knew that I HAD to do it.

I am grateful and humbled to know that many lives were challenged, uplifted, and encouraged along the way – all over the world. Some thought that I had shared "too much," and that may be so.... but I shared my story so that others who understand my journey will read it and relate – and will be assured that your past does not have to dictate your future.

Thank you for the many interviews and opportunities where I was invited to share with large and small audiences throughout the years. To make this Tenth Anniversary Edition special, I included a chapter to highlight where I am now in *"It's My Life"* journey.

Let us stay connected! My contact information is included on the last page of this book. Once you complete this book, I would love to hear from you!

Book Reviews

The piece on her mother impacted me significantly, especially since I am very close to my mother. I was also blessed by the fact that Michelle was able to transcend the various storms in her life with dignity and grace. She is faithful, committed and serving in the church, and one would never know her past pain.

-Bishop Donald Hilliard Jr., Senior Pastor
Cathedral International, Perth Amboy, New Jersey

Michelle, Michelle, Michelle, I just want to say THANK YOU for putting your life into print!!!!! We've had conversations before but sometimes as an avid reader it doesn't fully sink in until you read it. This book is truly an encouraging tool to me! I sat down and read for a good hour and finish it. I didn't want to put it down. May God continue to bless you to help bless someone else with your written words! Thanks again!!!!!!!!!

-Kakila Hunter, New Jersey

Very honest, open & genuine. Don't read it thinking you won't have to take a look in the mirror.

-Stella Cobbinah, New Jersey

When you have a book that is filled with so much LIFE, you cannot rush through it. I love to read and always have since I was little. This book was actually a "gift" to me and I will forever cherish it. The title was intriguing because where I am in life it was like the new woman's declaration! However, Michelle poured out her heart from page to page. I cried, laughed, and rejoiced throughout my reading. I appreciated each chapter that was colorfully written. I must take a trip to Jamaica as it was described beautifully in "Life in Jamaica". Michelle definitely captures the readers with her vivid stories. It was inspiring and encouraging to me all the way to the last page. I truly didn't want for it to end! Thank you for sharing your story Michelle. There is definitely MORE to hear concerning your story. Continue to live for God out loud, and know that your life is not in vain!

-Regina E Wilson, Texas

Almost finished your book....All I can say is wow! If we all revealed our testimony like that, this world would be better....We would have more compassion and caring for one another....I thank God for you and for your journey which is victorious in Him....

-Elaine Pretty, New Jersey

Truly profound and uplifting...I can truly relate to struggles in your marriage... Your book has certainly touched me to the core of my being and has allowed me to realise I am not alone with the struggles of being a Single Mom... By far my best job yet...Michelle thanks for your truly uplifting insight of your life and family. You have risen above adversity and become a strong black woman and for that I am truly grateful to know you and where you have come from and reached... Keep doing what you do and continue to be an inspiration for ALL women young & old.

-Anonymous Reader, Jamaica W.I.

As I read your book I could feel the special relationship you shared with your mother and grandmother. I've completed reading your very relevant and heartfelt work and it will help many.

-Cindy Williams Newsome, New Jersey

Michelle made me nostalgic for Jamaica as she remembers day to day life in JA...school days and the foods...oh the foods! She deals with relevant issues of today such as bullying, losing a loved one and heartbreak. Her story gives us hope. Hope that even though we may be going through the valley, there will be brighter days ahead and with Jesus as center of our lives we will emerge victorious, stronger and wiser. Thanks Michelle for sharing and saying the things that we don't always have the strength and courage to say. Thank you.

-Nikki Shakespeare, New Jersey

Table of Contents

Change Is Coming	1
Life in Jamaica	3
Emotional School Days - Childhood Reflections	7
Transition	13
College Life	19
Daddy Said, "I Do" - Again	25
Life After College	29
My Singleness "Ends"	31
Single Again	41
"It Is Well With My Soul"	47
Miracles In Abundance	51
Grandma	53
Moving Forward	55
My Life: Ten Years Later	57
Refective Prose Pieces From My Life	**61**
Your Net Woth	63
Personal Introspection	67
Truth - Today's Precious Commodity	71
So What's Normal Anyhow?	75
Superficiliaty in Friendships	77
The Split	81
Death by Comparisons	83
Growing Pains - Introspection	87
Grieving Loss	89
All Things Are Possible - Just Believe	93
Can You Forgive?	97
The Covenant	99
Want to Marry? Let God Choose!	103

Dedication

This book is dedicated to women everywhere who experienced situations that were difficult to verbalize to anyone else. Those moments of loneliness, grief and pain that you went through (or you are currently going through) are not in vain. I pray that the lessons I learned may penetrate your hearts, minds and souls, and will remind you that the darkest part of the night is just before dawn. Your new day is coming! Believe it, and don't give up.

To my family, thank you for loving me unconditionally. We have had our tough moments, but we are still together, loving and supporting each other as much as we can.

Lastly, I am dedicating my first book to the memory of my wonderful mother by launching this book on her birthday. She has left her indelible print on me physically (I have heard that I look and act a lot like her), and emotionally. Her strong Christian beliefs, teachings and character took hold of me at a young age. My life is forever transformed by my Mommy. "I will see you in heaven."

Continue to rest in Him, until we meet again.
(September 12, 1942 – March 19, 1989)

Foreword

Dr. Bernadette Glover
Executive Pastor, Cathedral International, Perth Amboy NJ

Behind the scenes, a rare breed can be found peering with intrigue at specks. Attentive to minute detail, they strain their eyes, quizzically pondering how to frame mystery and become acquainted with "what is", but still remain around the corner of understanding. The biologists see a documentary on the ocean in a drop of water; commentary on the body in a lock of hair. Specimens speak. "It's My Life – And I Live Here" is a specimen of reality.

Dr. Cicely Williams comprehended protein deficiency disease, Dr. Paula Tennant apprehended ringspot - a virus, and their yellow, black, green homeland soror in science has a grasp on life. Indeed, Ms. Cameron invites readers to come into focus about the properties of purposeful living. Faith in Christ, honesty, integrity, character, and heritage are the DNA of life. A good scientist tests deductions made from observations, a good mathematician renders analyses, informed certain projections, so also the author's introspection yields lessons, principles to be reckoned with.

A trail of wondrous grace can be found throughout "It's My Life – And I Live Here". Experience the trail as you walk through the pages that follow. You just might discover something of yourself along the way.

Why I Wrote This Book

You may be wondering why I decided to write this book. This project was birthed from years of blogging on social networks, initially as a way for me to work through several personal experiences. It started as a journal, which gained a huge following, and surprised me.

The experiences shared in this book are meant to show the reader how I overcame them and what I learned from each situation. The contents of this book are very personal, but they were carefully included without the intent to harm anyone. It is my desire for this book to reach many women (and men) so they can begin the process of healing from their past situations.

These are my memoirs, my experiences, my life, and all the individuals who played roles in each scenario. It's My Life and I Live Here. This is My Story.

Change is Coming

I knew I didn't want to leave Hughenden, my quiet, sprawling residential community in Saint Andrew. Hughenden stretched for at least 5 miles from end to end. Prefabricated bungalows in colorful hues, with low concrete walls, were (and still are) home for many nurses, teachers, policemen, company vice presidents, doctors and other professionals.

"WHY DID I HAVE TO LEAVE MY HOME???" I had begun to be interested in a boy who I grew up with (our parents were very good friends since before we were born), but did not see for several years because we attended different churches. We started "talking" when we were in our early teens, but our infrequent sightings of each other slowed the pace. He came to visit me for a "date" a few weeks before me and my sisters left. We exchanged addresses and pictures; he also did not want to see me leave. Life was good. Why mess up something good?

Yet, on the morning of Aug 25, 1988, I was placed in charge of my two younger sisters for our transition from Jamaica to the United States of America. The good ol' USA. 50 stars, 13 stripes, and so on. I missed my black, green and gold flag tremendously. I remember crying on the last day of high school as I sang the national anthem for the last time.

Life In Jamaica

There were so many reasons to love Jamaica! I grew up in the suburbs of Saint Andrew, which adjoins Kingston, the nation's capital.

After moving to the US, I would always be homesick for the cool breezes blowing through the mango trees, cherry trees, coconut trees, our ackee tree and hibiscus shrubs in our yard, the roosters crowing, pigeons cooing, dogs barking or cats meowing that could be heard in the distance. (Mating season was a KILLER!)

Even before I left for the United States, I knew I would miss the lazy summers; warm nights with crickets outside (and sometimes inside!), the smell of roasted breadfruit, callaloo, Jamaican Rum Cake at Christmas and the sound of the "salesmen" as they walked or rode by with their wares for sale. The "peanut man" was my favorite; roasted peanuts were kept warm in his portable steamer on the back of his bike. But what I would NOT miss was the mosquitos and frequent asthma attacks I experienced due to my severe allergic reactions to mango blossoms. Nor would I miss the frequent invasions from outdoor creatures into our house. I am a firm believer that what belongs outside should stay there.

Turns out, in some ways I also missed school. Our schools were highly disciplined; children would not dare to confront teachers unless they wanted their behinds to be worn out. Nowadays teachers are no longer allowed to spank children in school, but when I was growing up, that threat kept most of us in line. Many teachers did it out of genuine care and concern, but there were a few who took things way too far. Academics were rigorous and competitive. Our parents pushed us to perform to the best of our abilities. We were not allowed to slack off. That drive and determination has carried over into our adult lives. We are always determined to WIN.

I also missed my neighbors. My sister and I went with one set of neighbors to high school every morning. We would take the commuter bus home together in the evenings. My other next-door neighbor was one of my very best friends. I was 4 years older, but her maturity made it not matter too much. We played "pretend" by our backyard fence and talked about school, boys, and even our concerns about our lives. She is now a successful lawyer in Jamaica.

Life was so idyllic and quite predictable in Jamaica. Holidays were lots of fun. On random days relatives would stop by for no other reason than to be with us. Our home was a haven for many; life was difficult and the struggle to survive was great for most. We had our struggles, but favor followed our family. We were never hungry or in need of clothes or shoes. We did not eat what we wanted every day, but we were full every day. Our clothes may not have been stylish, but we were never naked or barefoot.

Many influential people were close to our family. My parents and my grandmother were greatly respected and revered by many pastors, bishops, other teachers, other policemen and so on. Our home was the venue for many important meetings, as we had a comfortable, enclosed patio where people could sit and discuss ideas. Mommy also held supplementary classes for her students on that patio. Pastors would visit and Grandma would prepare tea or coffee and they would marvel at the flavorful cup in their hands.

Food was the highlight of our home. Everything was freshly prepared or baked from scratch so we had the best nutrition we could afford. I remember seeing Grandma praying over a pot of food she was preparing. I really believe her prayers were the secret ingredients to her delectable dishes.

| *Life in Jamaica* |

Easter is a particularly huge celebration in Jamaica. My family would prepare roasted ham, with freshly baked bread from the bakery, callaloo (comparable to collard greens but softer and more flavorful), ackee (our national fruit with the consistency of scrambled eggs when prepared) and saltfish (salted and dried cod). There was curried goat, rice and peas (kidney beans or pigeon peas – but never both); jerk chicken or jerk pork; fricassee chicken, beef liver (which many people hated), mackerel "cooked down", meatballs (YUMMY!) and the list goes on. Black cake (a dark, delicious cake made with dried fruit that was soaked in wine) was usually baked for special occasions: weddings, Christmas and other serious celebrations. Everyday desserts would be pound cake, potato pudding, which has the consistency of pumpkin pie without the crust, and definitely ice cream and jello! Family members who we did not usually see would come by to share with us on major holidays. The laughter, and having good company over, made our holidays very special to us.

How I miss my childhood! I had my chores and hours of homework every day, but when all of those were completed, I had time to do anything I wanted. I loved (and STILL love) to read, so I devoured my mother's bookcase. "To Kill a Mockingbird", "Things Fall Apart", "1984", "Animal Farm", "Jane Eyre", "Wuthering Heights" and "The Adventures of Huckleberry Finn" were books I read at least once before I became a teen. Some ideas I did not grasp fully, but many of them I did. My mother's love for books was introduced to us at early ages. She loved the Arts as well. Through books and the arts our mother gave us a healthy dose of refined language and culture. Both were very important to her. She often corrected our grammar as we spoke and patois (the Jamaican dialect) was only allowed when we were in dramatic mode.

Music was also a big part of our lives. Jamaican music swirled all around us all day and night. Our radios and our neighbors filled the airwaves with reggae, soca and "lover's rock", a combination of R&B and reggae. I had

| **It's My Life** *and I Live Here* |

neighbors who were Bee Gees fans, so I got a taste of that once in a while as well (sometimes I would sneak in a dance or two on our front patio). Our exposure to all these different types of music was ironic, as we were raised in a very conservative Pentecostal home. No "secular" music was allowed – unless it was on the radio in-between regular talk-show programming or radio stories ("The Fortunes of Floralee" comes to mind). When the music came on we weren't allowed to participate – so the tunes would pound in our heads, but we could not sing or dance to them. Gospel was the only exception. My dad's Country Gospel and Christmas albums (vinyl records), were the extent of our music collection. Nat King Cole's "Christmas" is still part of my Christmas music collection today. I believe my family's conservative music restrictions affected me and my sisters in different ways. I still listen only to Christian music, but all genres – rap, rock, reggae, R&B, and so on. I think my sisters broadened their music tastes over the years to include "regular" R&B and other types.

     For all these reasons, the food, the music, the people, the way of life, I did not want to leave my island in the sun. I will always remember it fondly. We had a great life and a carefree childhood. That is what life should be all about!

Emotional School Days — Childhood Reflections

Things weren't all roses in Jamaica. When I began attending school in Jamaica as a little girl, I discovered that life was nothing like my safe cocoon at home. School toughened me significantly, but broke my heart in other ways. I was always shy in school - except with my friends. In fact, with them, the opposite would occur - I would talk their ears off! This non-stop chatter was not endearing me to many of my teachers. I endured many "stand, hands on your head and close your eyes" moments, and distinctly remember kneeling on hot concrete outside of my first-grade classroom because I just talked too much! Perhaps this was because I was bored in my classes. I was a straight A student in elementary school and mastered several classes in high school. (We do not have many junior high schools in Jamaica; most high schools begin at grade 7.) I loved to learn, but I don't think the teachers knew what to do with me so I would not become a nuisance. Many times other children would misbehave, and because they knew I was always getting in trouble, they would lie and get ME in trouble!!!

I shed bitter tears in school during my interactions with school mates. Several children targeted me as easy prey and I became the butt of their jokes. It did not help much that I wore thick, "coke-bottle" glasses and I was very chunky. I was also naïve at the time, and did not dare fight, so the other children had their way with me for years. There were days when I went home hungry from school, as other children raided my lunch box when I was not close by to guard its contents. Grandma's loving efforts to feed me well-balanced lunches often ended up in other children's tummies. I recall walking by a boy from an older grade and almost meeting the concrete face-to-face after he put his foot out to trip me so I would fall. Thankfully I saved my face from destruction, as well as a pair of glasses that would have cost a fortune to replace, had they been destroyed. The other students laughed as they watched me break my fall.

Although I had friends, I was far from being popular. My shyness and my overweight, asthmatic disposition made it difficult for me to shine in any other place but the classroom. Jamaica is known for its athletic prowess; those who did not have that skill were ridiculed mercilessly.

The tormenting from school mates did not end after I left elementary school. My quiet personality attracted loud, vicious girls in our all-girls' high school. They often played games with my personal belongings and hid them all over the school. This was all the more frustrating, because although teachers saw my plight, none stepped up to help. I cried constantly, but I was discreet with it because I knew if the girls knew how much their taunting affected me, it would bring on more of what I did not want. I was mortified when, in one instance, my homeroom teacher egged on the bullies in front of the entire class. As they teased me out loud from the back of the room (I sat in the front row), the teacher laughed and turned to me and said "You're gonna cry? You poor baby!" One girl, who sat next to me in homeroom, decided to stick up for me. She turned around to the teasers and said out loud "Why don't you all just leave her alone? What is your problem?" She was a fighter with a very loud mouth (and who did not take foolishness). The drama died down on that day. I was very grateful to her. She became my best friend for many years.

In the 9th grade, a lot of the tormenting died down as two of my main contenders were expelled. Still, a new set of individuals began to dig into my skin but I decided I would get them off my back once and for all; I became VERY sarcastic. I tested it out at first with one girl who laughed at my initial efforts at self-defense. We were standing in line, waiting to enter a class. I was standing behind her. She turned around and said: "You are such a square. You don't fit in at all!" my first sarcastic comment was "Well, then you are a circle!" After a while I was able to come back with a hot response anytime anyone bothered me. Interestingly enough, they began to respect me thereafter, especially after I embarrassed one of them who tried to make a fool out of me in front of a huge group of girls. I remember the moment and the emotions, not so much the topic of conversation. After being harassed in some sort of way, I fought back with my new silver tongue. Whatever it was that I said it must have been pretty surprising. The crowd erupted into a loud "WHOOOAAAA!!!!" in unison. Pleased with myself, I walked away proud and vindicated.

Being a Christian in school was TOUGH. When my peers discovered that I accepted Jesus Christ in the 8th grade (at 12 years old), they used that to tease me as well. I stood my ground, in that regard, and ignored them. I felt at peace with my decision to become a Christian, but a part of me longed to be able to "hang out" like everyone else could. I understood that my happiness was not to be based on what others thought of me or said about me. I knew my conscience was clear and I had the loving support of my family as I grew in my Christian faith. I also became friends with other Christians in school and would use those moments to "sharpen iron."

I remember being challenged by my best friend once. She came up in my face and asked me how is it I did not curse when I got angry. I told her because of Jesus living in me and because I wanted to keep pleasing Him I would not curse. She saw me get angry, but I did not use expletives to express myself. She faced off with me and shook me to get me to get angry and curse; I shrugged her off and walked away.

| It's My Life *and I Live Here* |

As the product of a very strict Christian home, there was always an internal struggle within me to do what was right (and what was expected) every day. I tried to live my life where I was still me, but I would only allow myself to go but so far (i.e. no cursing or lewd behavior). A part of me always wished that my upbringing was a bit more liberal, as I felt I had to censor my actions, words and even my thoughts all the time. I had that "Big Brother is watching you" feeling every day, and secretly wondered if anyone else felt that way too – and if they did not, why not?

I was also involved in the Inter-Varsity Christian Fellowship (IVCF) which allowed boys from our brother school to come onsite. I ALWAYS looked forward to our fellowships; we had a chance to check out the high school boys without having to do anything too crazy! We had great times together.

My incessant talking went with me to high school, but I was much busier in class then; there was too much work to do. So my talkative moments were usually during our jaunts from class to class, during lunch or other breaks or after school. One day, after school, as we sat under the mango trees, I decided to talk about any and every thing to get the attention of the popular girls. I started talking about my neighbors, who also attended my school. One of the girls who sat under the tree (my neighbor's friend) went back and told her what I said. That evening there was a knock on my mailbox outside. It was my neighbor. She threatened to beat me up for talking about her and her family at school. She came over wielding her hockey stick; she was very athletic and strong. I assured her that it would never happen again. I made a personal promise at that moment to stop speaking to others about everything. I basically kept that promise until just a few years ago. My conversations from that moment forward were concise (unless I was with family members or very close friends). I was almost silent with everyone else.

God has interesting ways of turning the tide. After dealing with persistent, merciless teasing for many years, I am here to report that many of those girls who participated are now professed believers in Jesus Christ. My then-best friend is now in ministry and she published a religious self-help book approximately two years ago. She is a regular church attendee and is pursuing an active role in ministry. All of this happened after she told me off a few years earlier by saying that it was not my business to preach to her about how she lived her life. (She was involved sexually with a man who visited her often, with her young son in the home.) I visited her to show her what I knew God wanted her to know; that He loved her and that she was better than that. She got very upset and hastily escorted me back to the train station so I could go back home. After her conversion she apologized and said "If I knew how free and clean I would feel after accepting Jesus Christ as my Savior, I would have done it a long time ago!" Those were the best words I had ever heard!

We have since lost contact with each other, but I still wish her all the best in her endeavors.

Transition

In 1983, Daddy left the Jamaica Constabulary Force (Police - Mobile Unit) for the U.S. to visit his uncle, who was a pastor. His visit never ended. Several months later we also said goodbye to Mommy. She had to be with her husband since they were joined at the hip and all. To make the transition a little easier for Grandma, who would now take care of me and my second sister full-time, Mommy took our youngest sister with her. She was only 2.

Grandma, my second sister and I lived together for 1 year. Our youngest sister returned to us within 1 year at age 3. I completed high school before I saw our mother again. My dad came to visit twice during those 5 years, but he only stayed for a few days each time. We had fewer people at home now, so we had more space and a teeny bit more freedom, but not really. Because Grandma was solely responsible for us, she had us on lock-down. We could go to school, church and that was it. No birthday parties. No barbeques. Not even gospel concerts – unless she took us there (and what fun is it to attend a concert with your grandmother?).

Since Grandma did not drive, we did not have a car. That meant we took the bus or walked everywhere we needed to go. We would get rides home from church almost every Sunday. If we left home early enough, we could hitch a ride on the church bus (of an affiliate church), which was basically a yellow school bus sent over from the U.S.

One night Mommy called to speak with Grandma. She told her that she had to have breast surgery. It sounded serious, but we didn't realize how serious it really was. When Mommy came to attend my high school graduation she sat us down and told us her story. She had breast cancer. It was so serious that they had to excavate bone and remove muscle and lymph nodes from her underarm. She lost all her hair and one breast. She did not tell us right away, but when I saw her for the first time after her surgery I could tell that she was not her usual self. Her skin was much darker than I remembered and her hair just didn't seem right. Later she allowed us to see that she was BALD! She was wearing a wig. I was terrified of the lady who I knew to be my mother, but seemed so unfamiliar. Was this REALLY my mom?

She had symptoms for several years, but did not seek medical attention in a timely manner. Those were the days prior to breast cancer awareness. Mommy realized she had a serious disease when Nancy Reagan had her double mastectomy. Her nipple had already inverted and was oozing by that point. My grandmother was devastated. Mommy was her only child. She was visibly upset and gave her daughter a piece of her mind (in a respectful way). She told her that she should have asked her some questions. Grandma had breast surgery earlier in life, but it was for a benign tumor. She said "When something does not look or feel right, see a doctor!" I am definitely following that advice.

So, on the afternoon of August 25th, we were greeted by our parents. We were very happy to be reunited once again. Five years of separation was OVER! Grandma was left behind in Jamaica to finalize our affairs. She sold furniture and Mommy's books. (Mommy taught English Literature at a vocational high school for many years.) As we got used to being together again and began adjusting to a new country, we anxiously awaited the arrival of our grandmother. September 1988 was a rough time for the Caribbean as Hurricane Gilbert tore through the area. Grandma's location was unscathed, but many people lost property and lives were lost. She was one of the more fortunate ones. My grandmother made it safely to the States on October 2.

| *The Transition* |

Mommy woke up not feeling well on the day before Grandma arrived. She complained of an intense headache and had trouble keeping food down. She went to see her doctor for a check-up and came back with terrible news; the cancer had spread! She now had tumors growing in her internal organs and in her brain. They were inoperable. She was back on chemotherapy and radiation again. Daddy had to take her for her treatments and she lost all desire to eat. Her complexion got very dark and she was irritable. We had to be quiet a lot so she would get some peace. Then Grandma told us her side of the story. She had felt the urge to come to the U.S. IMMEDIATELY from Jamaica, is what she told us. She knew she was needed, but she didn't know why. When she arrived and learned of my mom's new diagnosis she realized that she would be taking care of us again – as well as her only child.

This went on until March 1989. Mommy came home from the doctor in early March with news that made my heart stop: She was DYING. The doctors gave her 2 weeks to live. They asked her if she wanted to go back to Jamaica, but she told them that her family was here now so no, she would stay here. When she told us the news we were shaken. The house got very quiet. I got up and ran into our room and locked myself in and PRAYED. AND PRAYED. AND PRAYED. I was only 16! My sister was only 15 at the time, and the youngest was only 8! My birthday was March 21st. I wondered what would happen by then.

Mommy began shutting down. She started to refuse food and drank very little. She slept most of the time and snored heavily. She started to retain fluid (edema). I remember it like it was yesterday. On Thursday, four days before her departure from this life, she took one hour to drink a cup of warm milk. That was her last meal. She lay down across the bed ever so slowly and fell asleep. I stayed with her that night as Daddy had gone to his new job. (Mommy had found that job for him right before her final prognosis.) I left her that morning to go to school. I told her to sleep well. I did not know that would be the last time she would be home with us. Grandma called the ambulance for her after she sent us off to school. She knew she was not okay as she did not stir, but kept snoring loudly. She responded slightly to her mother's voice but did not wake up. Mommy was in a coma.

The next day, Saturday, we stopped by the hospital to visit on our way to work (we had part-time jobs). The room smelled foul. I was told later that was the smell of death. Her mouth was wide open as she gasped for air. Her liver was swollen, so it pushed up against her lungs. I leaned over to her and whispered in her ear: "I'll see you in heaven." She moaned loudly in response. I had heard somewhere that the last of our senses to go is our hearing. I know she heard me loud and clear.

On Sunday, March 19, 1989, on Palm Sunday at approximately 5pm, Mommy slipped out of her pain-racked body into the arms of an angel. She was escorted Home. We received a call after the coroner pronounced her dead. Someone asked us if we wanted to visit. My sister that followed me and I went to see her. Daddy was already there; he leaned up by the doorway of her room with blood-shot eyes. He was probably crying. After all, he loved her for so many years. They were married for 20 years. My grandmother's twin sister had come from Canada a few days before, so she sat in the room staring in disbelief at her favorite niece's body. I walked up to Mommy and touched her head. I said out loud "Her hair was just beginning to grow back." She was still warm, but she was beginning to get stiff. Her mouth was still wide open, but no air came in or out. One tear ran down her right cheek. She was crying as she departed.....

I had not cried yet.

On Monday, March 20th, the ministers and family friends were coming over to plan the funeral services. I decided I was going to school. My sisters

| *The Transition* |

followed my lead. I thought it was better to get out of the house than to listen to them do that. When we got to school we all fell apart in our classrooms. I clearly remember my homeroom teacher saying: "Okay everyone, pipe down! Michelle lost her mother over the weekend. She is going to say something and we will all pray for her." (I attended a Christian school.) The classroom went silent immediately, and everyone's mouths dropped wide open and their eyes bulged at the news. I stood up and began to tell everyone what had transpired since October. I always asked for prayers, but I never said exactly what was wrong with my mother. On that day they heard it all. My teacher began to pray as I started to cry. My cries became audible, so one of my friends led me out of the classroom to the bathroom. As I left my classroom, I saw the same scene occurring with my sisters in the hallway. I was very sad and confused. I thought we were coming to America to live happily ever after! What happened to that dream? God, why didn't you save her from dying? The teachers were devastated. They did what they could to support us. We went to school every day; I could not stand to be home without my mother.

Tuesday, March 21st, was just another day to me. I was now 17. This was only 2 days after my mother departed this life. My class wondered what to do to help me get through this bewildering time so they planned a surprise birthday party for me. I was very moved by their thoughtfulness, but I could not enjoy it. They knew that, but they could not think of what else they could do for this new, bewildered immigrant girl, who had just lost her mom.

On Saturday, March 26th, we laid Mommy to rest. My younger sister and my then-best friend, who was also close to Mommy, sang a song with me without any of us breaking down in tears. And I will never forget "ashes to ashes, dust to dust" at the graveside. I stood over her coffin and dropped the roses on top. I felt as if I was rooted in place. My other sister had a wild look in her eyes so someone quickly moved her away from the graveside. I wanted so badly to be left alone for a while so I could think. Mommy, why NOW?

| **It's My Life** *and I Live Here* |

Why, when I was ready to reconnect, to laugh, to love and to share my every thought with you? Why did you have to go NOW? You do know we love you a lot, right? WHY didn't you get your breast checked by a doctor when you first felt the lump?

Before she died, Mommy sat us down and gave us a moving lecture. We were told that at age 30 we had to begin mammograms. We were to do self-checks every month and to take care of our bodies. She said "I wasted my life! I have so many things I wanted to do, and now I will never do them." I haven't forgotten that speech, so now I'm writing this book. This is one of the things I have always wanted to do. I must push out all that is within me to fulfill my destiny.

College Life

After Mommy's death, various people came into our lives to try to tell us what we needed to do and how to do it. They also tried to discourage me from going to college right away. I graduated again from high school here. (In Jamaica we graduate at the end of 11th grade. I came here and attended the 12th grade and graduated again.)

I had applied and was accepted to the only college I considered because of the expense in applying to other colleges, and because my best friend at the time was also planning to attend – so we could be roommates! It was located in up-state NY, approximately one and a half hours away from home. I earned scholarships and grants and took out some student loans to cover expenses. I was also involved in the college work-study program to assist with paying for school. As a freshman I had to clean toilets and bathroom mirrors, vacuum hallways and dust stairwell banisters. How fun.

Because of built-up tension from previous life events, I did not fully apply myself to studying as I should. I went out A LOT to bowling alleys and other late-night trysts with new-found friends, leaving little time for studying. My freshman grades were reflective of my excessive social life, and they never fully recovered. I also remember one night in my freshman year when I broke down totally. I was frustrated and really missed my mom. I screamed, cried and shouted all evening; my roommate left the room for a long time. After I was emotionally spent, I went on my knees and poured out my hurting heart to God. I told Him that I did not fully understand why Mommy had to go so soon, but I knew that He has plans for all of us and that He would take care of us. I felt a heavy burden lift from my shoulders when I got up off my knees. That was the second time I allowed myself to cry over my mother's death.

Next year, 1990, was the time for my sister to graduate from high school and join me in college. People strongly dissuaded her from coming by saying she should stay behind and attend community college and work somewhere to help Daddy earn income. I fought for her to join me because I knew Mommy, an educator, would have turned in her grave if that had ever happened. Children are not adults; children must be allowed to live out their dreams, no matter what happens. When we force children to help adults maintain their dreams we raise resentful, angry children. At the young age of 18 I knew that already.

So I was a sophomore and she was a freshman.

We were proud of our alma mater. While I was in high school, a representative from the college had come to visit. I decided right then and there that I would attend this small Christian college in some far-away place I'd never even heard of.

Life on campus was very interesting. I think the culture shock and recovery really took place while I attended college. I made some fascinating friends; I knew star basketball athletes, science gurus and nursing students who were enrolled in the dual-college program with Pace University. One aspiring hair professional would cut and curl my hair in the dorm hallway every few weeks. She was Caucasian, which made it more interesting. My asymmetrical, perfectly coiffed bob was the result of her patient work.

We were financially strained at home, so while we attended college we depended on the benevolence of my roommate for commuting to and from school during breaks. As an only child, she had the privilege of receiving her own car shortly after we began college. She was also my best friend at the time. We talked A LOT about almost everything. She was very dependable and would come to my rescue on various occasions. Unfortunately as time went on, she realized I was not able to offer as much as she had offered to me. My chief purpose at school was to graduate, and I had planned to do so in the least burdensome way possible. I was not lazy, but the luxuries of life were not a priority for me. They certainly were a priority for my roommate. Soon I was unable to watch TV as I desired, and so on – just because it wasn't my TV. After handling these unfortunate scenarios one time too many, we parted ways in our senior year. I found a roommate with similar priorities; like me, she just wanted to finish in a "no-frills" fashion.

My best friend experiences taught me that everyone will not agree with my views, my life-choices or my priorities. Not everyone will be willing to compromise or change just because their circumstances have changed. It took a while for me to understand this, but I am better for learning this lesson. I have learned to embrace others even when it is difficult for them to accept me.

Biology was my first choice for my college major. As far back as I could remember I wanted to be a doctor, hence my major. Science had always fascinated me as a child. In college I loved learning anatomy, physiology and other related courses. Math came naturally to me as well, so Calculus was also part of my world. Soon I was able to transition from toilet-scrubbing to assisting in a lab for the remainder of my time in college. I was in charge of the frogs that were shipped to us for Human Physiology class. They were our "guinea pigs" (poor things) for lab experiments. They were used to demonstrate how muscles worked and for dissections - that was their sole purpose. I also graded lab tests and assisted underclassmen with lab experiments. I LOVED IT! I learned the value of staying with difficult and mundane tasks, which allowed me to be promoted to do more interesting work which was related to my major.

While academically I was thriving, my romantic life had its ups and downs. Shortly before I attended college, I met and fell head over heels for one of my best friends' cousins. It was so serious that we began to discuss marriage. But there was one HUGE problem: our educational levels were not equal. He was very gentlemanly and considerate and would shower me with many gifts, but he was not in school like I was. We were ridiculed as being mismatched and after MUCH pressure from my family I had to break it off with him. I felt like something had died inside of me when I had to walk away. He mourned the end of our relationship and remained single for a long time (as in YEARS) thereafter. (sigh)

After the end of that relationship I became involved with another man on campus. He left PLENTY to be desired, but I thought he genuinely cared about me so I went along with the relationship. He was a smooth talker. I thought he loved me because we spent so much time together, but when he began pressuring me for sex (and it almost occurred), I realized that he did not have my best interest in mind. That relationship ended and I remained single until after I graduated.

Staying in college was not easy. My dad was unable to support me and my sister financially. He would call sometimes, but he was unable to do much more. He was limited by the mountain of medical bills that my deceased mother had left behind. Thankfully, some of the doctors understood our plight and forgave much of the debt. Life was very hard. I remember needing to take out yet another student loan, but this one had to be paid during college. That was one of the toughest decisions I had to make, but it was necessary. I also remember, at the beginning of my final semester of my senior year, that I went into the bursar's office and discovered that they were sending me home if I was unable to pay my contribution towards my tuition. I burst into tears because I was too close to the finish line to quit! I promised myself that I would graduate from college within four years, mainly because of the expense in staying longer. The bursar quietly brought out a donor letter and gave me an address. She said "Write this person and tell him thank you. His donation will pay for your semester." I could not tell anyone about it (except my family members, of course). I was amazed because it was unexpected! I was indeed grateful and thanked the donor profusely. Thankfully, this was my last time trying to figure out (financially) how to finish college within four years!

Daddy said, "I Do" - Again

After Mommy's death, Daddy was despondent, but functional. Although he was grieving he still got up every day to take care of his children and his mother-in-law. After some time we noticed some significant changes; he began to speak very negatively and angrily to us. Sometimes I wondered what he thought of us. He never had to handle us directly before Mommy died. Grandma and Mommy made sure that we were kept in order, and that all our needs were supplied ever since we were all born. Daddy worked and the ladies did everything else. While growing up in Jamaica, we were also sheltered from learning how to run a household. My parents hired help to clean, wash and occasionally cook for us. We did our chores on weekends – the high-maintenance ones such as wiping down the refrigerator (inside and out), cleaning down the seemingly millions of glass window panes and glass doors on our patio and dusting book shelves. As for daily meal preparation, I only went as far as preparing breakfast items. This sheltered lifestyle did not change much when we transitioned to the United States, so when I cooked my first chicken after Mommy's death I was embarrassed (and in tears) when Daddy cut his piece of chicken and blood poured out onto his plate. I was 17 years old at the time.

After Mommy's death, Grandma had planned on living with us "forever", just as she had been doing since my mother and father first got married. This was not to be. Three years later, while we were home on a break from college, a letter came in the mail from Jamaica that changed everything for us. Daddy was newly engaged to another lady, which meant Grandma had to move on. Daddy had met the lady of his dreams on one of his visits to Jamaica. He was formally introduced to her by a bishop and his wife, with an initial suggestion from a church mother in NJ. After they discussed the possibility of a relationship and spent some time together, they decided to pursue a long-distance courtship. Daddy flew to Jamaica a few times to visit her, or she visited him in NJ on one of her many trips abroad. After a short while they decided to get married.

My grandmother cried for days over that letter as she had not envisioned a separation from us. We had never lived apart, except for those two months between our transitions to the United States, in 1988. My heart was broken. We were away in college and our youngest sister was about to start middle school. What would happen to her? If Grandma had to move out and live somewhere else, who would take care of our youngest sister when Daddy went to work, since he worked the night shift?

After Grandma dried her tears she sought help from church members for a place to stay. One family offered her a room. She was comforted in knowing that she would be able to be around people who were familiar to her, but she missed being with us. After a while, she found a live-in job during the week and went back to her little room on weekends. She paid rent to the church people who owned the house and gave us most of the money she saved. She paid bills on our behalf and bought my first car. She was paid well to take care of a 90+ year old woman. The lady loved Grandma's caring spirit. Grandma would continue to work until she retired from another position at the age of 82.

When my sisters and I met my father's fiancé for the first time, we were very skeptical. She looked NOTHING like our Mom and she definitely didn't act like her. We already had a huge chip on our shoulders because we saw her as the cause of Grandma's departure. It took all of us a VERY long time to get used to her.

Their wedding was held in Jamaica. My sisters and I flew down to attend. It was very lavish, as she owned a thriving medical private practice. The who's who in government, religion and medicine were all privileged to attend.

Once she sold her practice and moved to NJ to live with Daddy and us, we realized that it would soon be time for all of us to spread our wings. Life was just too different with our stepmother living with us, and we thought it would be easier for us to move on with our lives.

Returning to school was a welcomed diversion from all the changes happening at once. During my senior year, my sister and I lived next door to each other in the dorms. I saw her occasionally and checked in on her to see how she was doing. We were both Bio majors, so we had a few classes together. Over the summer before her junior year (which was my senior year) she met and started dating a young man who lived not too far from campus. He was not a student from our school; in fact I do not think he was in school at all. As time went on I felt impressed to speak to her about him. I felt uncomfortable with their relationship, because I was afraid that she would lose focus on why she was in school in the first place.

My suspicions were valid. On the week of my college graduation, I received news: my sister was pregnant. I was DEVASTATED. I cried out in agony. I felt hurt. We were already struggling to make ends meet and the surprise of her pregnancy would only make her struggle that much harder. I also wondered how this would impact her academically, since our college did not allow women to attend if they conceived outside of marriage. I felt helpless, as I was unable to protect her from such situations. My sister was staying on campus for graduation, as she was on the school choir. When she received confirmation of her pregnancy, she packed her things and moved off-campus. We (our family and my former roommate) did not know exactly where she was. I prayed like a maniac as I prepared for graduation. I was able to get calls through to her and I pleaded for her to move back on campus. I begged her to come to my graduation even if she was unable to sing on the school choir. Conversations like "Sis, please come back on campus! I really want you to be at my graduation, even if you won't be able to sing on the choir. Please....." and her responding: "I don't know if I will make it. I will see what happens," made me feel helpless.

On graduation day, I was in knots. I was concerned about much more than the actual event; my sister's safety and the welfare of her unborn child were my priority. I also wondered if she would come. When my sister arrived at my graduation, I felt a lot better. I felt as if things would only get better from that moment forward. On that day I sang to a large audience for the first time. My year-long vocal classes prepared me to sing "Daystar," (as sung by the Brooklyn Tabernacle Choir) as a solo, to an amazed student body, faculty and their family members.

Later that day, after all the photos were taken and the caps and gowns were packed away, my former roommate and I found my sister's new place. Her unborn child's father was not home at the time, so we quickly grabbed her belongings and told her we weren't leaving for New Jersey without her. She reluctantly agreed to come home with us. I am thankful that she did. Five months later she gave birth to a beautiful little girl. Now I cannot imagine what life would have been like without my niece.

Life After College

I graduated with a Bachelor of Arts in Biology in May 1993, with no special honors to boast about. My initial dream of becoming a doctor was addressed by my advisor and professor; he told me that my grades would probably make it difficult for me to pass the MCATs. I believed what he said and changed my focus from becoming a doctor. In hindsight I realized that I had allowed someone to decide FOR ME what I would do with my life. The effect of that one conversation played out in my life for a long time.

Immediately after I graduated, I realized that I probably made an error in choosing a small private college. We did not have work-life counseling or orientation available for new or upcoming graduates. When I was told I needed to generate a resume, I had NO IDEA what to do. I was not coached on interviewing for jobs, so I had the most difficult time landing work.

Because I had previous experience in the fast food industry, I was able to take on a job working at Nathan's Famous. I was quickly promoted to supervisor, but I was bored and impatient. I had a four-year college degree working at a place where mostly high school students, or others who did not have advanced degrees, worked.

I stayed at Nathan's for approximately 3 months. I quit in January 1994, to begin orientation as a bank teller for a major banking corporation. I was great at Math, so I thought it would be a breeze. I was unprepared for the intense two-week paid training on the responsibilities of a bank teller – such as learning accounting terms and how to process checks, and so on. It was a very challenging training period. When I passed, the trainer said "I did not know you would pass. Congratulations!" What!?

It was tough transitioning from biology labs to preparing and selling fast food to conducting financial transactions, but I made it work the best I could. I worked hard in whatever capacity I found myself in, but I never settled for menial tasks. I always strove for challenging assignments. If none were available or forthcoming, I would seek opportunities elsewhere. The due date for my student loans was imminent; it was time to make monthly payments. I was determined not to be a burden to Daddy, since we were now all back home with an extra person to care for (i.e. my baby niece).

My Singleness "Ends"

Shortly after graduating from college, I began noticing a tall, dark young man who sang the lead in another church's choir. I was part of a church organization that enabled churches from different locations to convene regularly with other churches. His church happened to be one of them.

I was also singing solos frequently by then. Every time a church event would take place, I was scheduled to represent our local congregation. I logged many miles to and from concerts, fund-raising rallies and other special church services so I could sing my soul out for Jesus. One day I decided that I wanted to connect with various people within the church organization, since I was away at college for four years. I began waving friendly hi's and goodbyes to the tall, dark young man. He noticed and responded by smiling and waving in return. I thought he was very friendly and approachable. One day, I went upstairs to the audio-visual area where he recorded the church services and began speaking to him. He gave me his phone number. I felt like I was on cloud nine! Soon we began dating.

I learned that his brother was a minister and his sister-in-law was an awesome singer (and comedienne) too! Soon I met extended family members and began hanging out at his home when his mom was there. Before long, I fell head over heels for this man. His charming, funny personality pulled me in.

Because of my caring personality I started investing heavily in this man. I paid for things I probably should not have covered as a woman. In retrospect, I realize that he did very little for me in return. I felt secure in our relationship as he seemed very much "into me" when we were together, so my assumption was that we shared the same feelings for each other. I began to trust him more and more.

After we dated for three years and six months, I sensed that something was happening. We had looked at wedding rings and decided what style to buy, and so on. As my 25th birthday approached, my father began saying some interesting things, like I was "spreading my wings," statements that made me think. Did he know something I did not know?

On the night of my birthday my boyfriend took me to Medieval Times. That was my first experience there. As the jousting contest took place, he took my left hand and slid the ring on. I was stunned. I was engaged! Just like that! (Honestly, I was disappointed. I thought he would go down on one knee and ask me to marry him as I saw on TV so many times.) I went to the ladies' room to admire the ring I just received. Finally, I made the connection with my father's interesting sayings: he had asked my father for my hand in marriage earlier and my dad knew which day he was going to propose.

One night after we became engaged, I needed to speak to "John" (not his real name) about something and I could NOT find him! I decided to get dressed and I drove 30 minutes away to see if I could locate him. I never found him, but eventually he returned my call. I berated him for being out late at night without giving me a heads-up on what he was about to do. He was quick to give an explanation that I "bought". He said he had to help one of the church sisters move into her new place. I was somewhat suspicious (as in "Who moves someone into an apartment at 12 midnight?"), but I decided to accept the explanation without further questioning. This type of scenario would play out a few times between us during our time of dating and engagement but I did not give it serious thought. If I thought about it, I rationalized his behavior.

| *My Singleness "Ends"* |

One month before we were due to marry he made a confession to me about another woman. I was so upset that I gave him back the engagement ring and told him not to call me. He begged me to forgive him and take him back. Multiple floral arrangements arrived with teddy bears and other trinkets. These were followed by pleading phone calls from him, his minister-brother and his mother. Everyone pointed out that he "made a mistake". They insisted it was "just a mistake". My heart was uneasy, but I talked myself into believing what I was told. After all, we all make mistakes at some point, right? I had prayed and fasted for that entire month. I finally believed that marrying him was my answer.

I was not nervous on my wedding day in 1997. I should have been. It was my first marriage and I was only 25. I was also a virgin. In retrospect, I think I had EVERY reason to be nervous. The ceremony went through without a hitch. I know he was very happy to know he had caught a prize that was 13 years younger.

On our first day and night together, I noticed that he was very controlling and dictating by the way he ordered me around and belittled me if I did not do what he wanted immediately. Soon I realized that I would have very little freedom to breathe in this relationship. I realized immediately that I had married the wrong person, but I was willing to stick it out and remain faithful to the covenant. I longed for a relationship in which I felt valued and loved. I tried many times over our 8 years together to reach out for meaningful dialog, but it usually ended in painful arguments that sometimes lasted for days. He never forgot anything I ever said, so any discussion would reference words spoken months before – in or out of context. Whenever he was angry, he would put on his boots really fast, slam the front door, slam his car door and speed off down the driveway to God knows where. John's behavior took its toll on me. I was depressed and moody most of the time.

My husband and I rarely spent time together. He selected a job with the flexibility of daytime or evening/night hours and he always chose evening/night. We were like passing ships. The only time we were home together was when I decided to stay home from work on Mondays, one of his days off, or when we would go to church on Sunday mornings. Sunday morning was the only time I saw him wear his wedding band; it was off all the other times. Whenever I asked why he wouldn't wear it, he always had an excuse, such as it was too big, it would get bent or lost, and so on.

Our marriage took an unexpected turn in the year 2000. I was in our home, minding my own business, when I looked down and saw a tiny piece of paper on the carpet. I picked it up and began to unfold it. To my horror, it was a newspaper ad to an adult entertainment location in a far-away town, with handwritten directions along the side, in HIS handwriting. I was so floored by what I found, I started to cry. Shortly thereafter I received mail addressed to someone who did not live there. I looked at the envelope and recognized the telephone number in the top-left corner of the letter. (I memorize phone numbers, sometimes unintentionally.) I reached for our phone bill and saw that same phone number and realized that my spouse had given them a fictitious name, possibly so that I would not suspect that he was involved in anything that he knew I would be against. I had a feeling I would see something inside that I did not need to see, but I opened the envelope anyway. The explicit contents of women posing in suggestive positions made me feel very ill. I went to the shredder and destroyed them but I kept the envelope to use as evidence to initiate a conversation later. When I confronted him with hard evidence about the envelope and the pictures of the women (that I had destroyed), he still lied. I asked why bother to lie when it was so obvious that the pictures were ordered by him (as shown by our home phone bill)? I never received a clear answer to my question.

These incidents were the beginning of sorrows for me. I was married to a sex addict who was used to living life on his terms. His addiction to pornography ran deep; phone sex was his "thing." Sexual trysts were familiar past-times for him. He always wondered how I knew when he stepped out on our marriage, but I always knew. His behavior would change; he would stay away from me. Attempts at intimacy became stressful and unfulfilling. I was miserable. I tried to put on a front for family and church members because I did not think they would care enough, or could do anything to help me in my plight. After we had several discussions with pastors and with my dad, my husband gave me the impression that he had "changed," but I know better now. No-one (except God) can change a deep-rooted addiction overnight. All he did, each time, was find a slicker way to continue his habits and practices. John brought home X-rated magazines from work. I threw them in the garbage every time I found them. He taped X-rated cable shows onto video tapes; I found many of them and had them destroyed.

One thing that was disconcerting for me was the feeling of being a prisoner in my own home. We had purchased a house together immediately after we got married, and I was burdened with the pressure of keeping up with all the bills and keeping it clean. I was also expected to cook often and so on, but with little help from him in return. I would come in tired from work and attempt to "make it happen" in the kitchen. It was an exhausting enterprise and soon I felt that the house was a huge burden on me emotionally, financially and even mentally. Soon I dreaded going home. He also prevented me from displaying my creativity there. I made several attempts to beautify our home and he would object to every suggestion. I started to die inside.

My husband's controlling nature was so bad that it got to the point where my family and friends felt unwelcome in our home. Whenever I invited anyone over, or if family members dropped by, and he found out, thereafter he would grill me: "Who came here?" My response was always: "I am not having an affair. If I am being faithful to the marriage it shouldn't concern you who came by." I was careful not to have any male visitors - except my father

- when my spouse was not around. Sometimes my sisters would visit, but not often.

God, was I lonely! I learned first-hand how much our decisions really determine where we end up and what we experience.....

One thing that made me very uncomfortable at home was all the cameras that were set up strategically around our home. Some faced the front entrance, enabling us to see who was coming up the street long before they arrived at our doorway. Worse yet, a video tape ran the entire time he was away from home, so he was able to see who came to our house when he was not there. Every time John came home, he grilled me about "Who came today?" I knew he wanted to keep tabs on my life and on what I was doing. After a while, I felt uncomfortable even holding a conversation on my home phone. I was paranoid because of all the unreasonable actions of my husband, but was made to feel as if my paranoia was all in my head. I felt deep down that I was being watched as I moved throughout our home. I couldn't believe that my privacy was being invaded by someone who had declared that he "loved me" in front of over 300 people, in 1997. I couldn't help but wonder, Is this what real love looked like?

There were financial troubles too. When we purchased the house, we only paid half of its value since it was a foreclosed home. The payments were manageable initially, but after a while, I felt we were always behind the eight-ball in an attempt to keep the bills current. I took on an extra job to help close the gap, but my spouse had no intentions of doing any more than he thought was necessary to keep things afloat. Financially, the burden laid squarely on my shoulders.

After the initial infidelity incidents, things had begun to improve in the marriage (or so I thought), so I became pregnant in early 2002. Shortly after I conceived many things changed. I had to surrender my part-time job because I felt faint from standing for so many hours. I had to work a modi-

| *My Singleness "Ends"* |

fied shift at my full-time job, as I had extreme edema and my legs became huge and heavy when I sat for too long. Despite all the physical changes that I was experiencing due to the pregnancy, I was still expected to do everything alone at home. I was still grocery shopping for us when I was about 6 months pregnant. I was irritated and frustrated. The next time we ran out of food I declared, "YOU are going food shopping. You gobble down the food and expect me to replace it right away. If you plan to eat, you need to get to the store." John was LIVID, but I would not budge. He had to go to the grocery store for the duration of my pregnancy. He brought up "how unfair it was" for him to have to shop for groceries several times for the remainder of my pregnancy, and even when our son was born. I ignored him every time.

During my pregnancy, I noticed that he was no longer as interested in me romantically. After much prayer about the matter, I realized he had been stepping out of the marriage regularly during those 9 months. I confronted him on the matter and there was a deafening silence. He confessed that he was involved with women during my pregnancy. After dealing with that crushing blow, I set the issue aside (for the time being) and waited to give birth. Our son was born in November of 2002. I felt so lonely during the delivery.

While I was recovering from my delivery, one indiscretion totally changed my mind toward my husband. He made a sexual advancement towards one of my close relatives, in our home, while I was waiting to be discharged from the hospital with our baby! I was beyond livid, as I felt betrayed during what should have been a happy, bonding moment between us and our new baby. In my mind, no-one or nothing else should have mattered. I prayed for God to release me from this bondage labeled as marriage.

As our son grew up, it was evident to me that his father was using him as a pawn to manipulate me and our relationship. I was mortified, as he was an innocent child with no control over who his parents were or how he was born. There were mornings when I had to get up and get our son ready for daycare, drop him off, and then go to work while he slept in because I disagreed with him on an issue the night before. Pain was etched deep inside my soul. I cried myself to sleep often. My spouse would sleep on the sofa after watching porn until the wee hours of the morning. I was very depressed and longed for happiness and true love. After some time, I did not care whether or not sex occurred. Nevertheless, I was determined to do what was right, so I never cheated on him.

    My anger ran deeply. There were nights when he chose to sleep in our bed (he spent most nights on our sofa), and I was tempted to get either his machete (which he kept on his side of the bed), or a kitchen knife and kill him in his sleep. I knew, though, that I would have left our son without parents (as I would have been jailed for life), so I prayed, cried and asked God for a way out of the madness.

    I spent a lot of money in the gynecologist's office on periodic HIV and STD testing. Thankfully they all came back negative every time. I was only diagnosed with frequent yeast infections, which were treatable and curable.

    When our son was two years old, we were arguing and shouting almost daily. I saw the effects on him; he began to regress. One day after my spouse and I had had a horrible fight, our son curled up on our sofa and sucked his fingers with a blank stare on his face. On that day, in that moment, I decided it was time to leave. I was taking him with me because I wanted to ensure that he had a good role model and a stable environment - as stable as any single mother could provide for her child. Soon I began shopping around for an apartment and rented a post office box. We also went to see another pastor for counseling one last time. During the session, my spouse only pointed out that he was angry that I told people about his porn addiction. At the time of the initial discovery, I had called some ministers and other people, whom I trusted and respected, and I told them of my discovery because I was scared and confused. Five years later, he was still bringing it up!

The last counseling attempt had no lasting effect and nothing positive came out of it. I began moving ahead with plans to relocate.

One rainy fall night in 2005, I looked at the house one last time. I had poured a lot of finances (and went into significant debt) by repairing the roof, installing vinyl siding, installing new windows throughout the entire house, and renovating the basement. Now I had to walk away from all of that. I told myself that my peace of mind and sanity were worth much more than the thousands of dollars I invested in repairing the house.

When my spouse got back home from work that night, he began calling around to try to find me. My family members were not informed that I had moved out. When they finally discovered what I did, they tried to encourage me to return, but I never did - except once, when I went to get some items I had left behind by mistake. The house alarm came on because he changed the door locks, which is illegal if the other person's name is still on the deed. I knew the police were on their way, so I left quickly. Since the alarm company called to advise him of the "break-in," he soon called me, wanting to find out if it was a burglar, or if it was "just me." I was mortified at the call, but I responded graciously. I began to realize that it would not be up to me to punish him for all the wrongs I experienced at his hands. God would take care of him.

Within a few months, it was time to sell the house. John pressured me to continue to pay the mortgage, since my name was also on the deed, but I assured him that I had my own bills to pay, and I was in no position to support two households. He refused to pay, even though he lived there for almost one year after I moved out. To avoid foreclosure, I worked with the bank to force him to sell. We made very little profit on the sale, due to his refusal to sign a contract with previous potential buyers. It was one of the most stressful times I had ever experienced with him. Trying to come to an agreement about visitation and child support payments for our son proved stressful as well. Because I knew John was addicted to sex, I felt VERY uncomfortable leaving our son in his care, without supervision. When he approached my close relative during my recovery from childbirth, I suspected he was doing unmentionable things to our son as well, so I prevented him from seeing his son without supervision for over 1 year. (He did not speak well yet so he was unable to tell me if anything unusual had happened to him.) After that year, he was only allowed same-day visits (no overnights), for at least another 6 months.

I was bitter. And I was VERY angry. I was angry with myself because I hadn't seen this coming earlier. Why didn't I heed my inner promptings, one month before our wedding, to go ahead and cancel?

I had given all my youth to a man who did NOT love me. I gave my virginity to someone who took it as just another notch on his belt; that's how I felt. What I valued was thrown in my face over and over. He laughed and mocked my relationship with God, which confused me since we had met in church, and he had been very involved in church events (singing, audio-visual work, and driving the church van). It was then that I realized it was just a set-up that was used to trick and entrap a real (and naïve) Christian woman. I stood firm in my beliefs. I know in retrospect that my salvation and strong relationship with God kept my mind from being shattered. I was ridiculed for buying relationship books and listening to relationship help talk shows on Christian radio. I prayed and fasted regularly for our marriage, but if God did not join us together, how could He keep us from going asunder?

Single Again

In March 2007, the judge brought the gavel down, ending 9.5 years of misery. I felt like a load had rolled off my shoulders. I took action immediately to revert to my maiden surname. It hurt having to file for divorce, but I felt that if I did not, he would have drained me dry and left me empty inside. In fact I had already felt that way, but it would have progressed to become worse.

I had already decided that I would marry again and immediately started taking steps to prepare for the next individual. This time, I told myself, I would be ready, and I would be more discerning.

Life as a single parent, raising a precocious boy, has not been easy. He has been strong-minded since the day of his birth. We are similar in our temperaments, which I believe is the foundation of our friction at times, but we love each other dearly. I know that I could not go anywhere without him for more than a day or two and not feel a hole within my heart. I remember the days when he used to run away from me – as a test, I am sure. He was only 3 or 4, so he was still quite young. He thought we were having a fun chase as my heart pounded for fear that he would run out into traffic. Could I catch him in time??? He was a master running machine (and is still so today), so that was a challenge. Thankfully God's merciful presence kept my fears from being realized.

One incident that is forever branded in both of our memories was when he wandered away from our apartment complex and ended up in a townhouse community next door. Someone saw him wandering around and called the police. I called the police in a panic, after trying to find him for fifteen minutes. They told me where I could find him, so I ran out to get my son. A burly, African-American cop went over to my son and observed me approach him. My son was upset because he did not know where he was and he had not seen me for a few minutes. When he saw me, he was already frenzied, so he had a full-fledged meltdown. The cop became suspicious and assumed that my son ran away because I had been abusing or neglecting him. I tried to explain that he was outside playing with our neighbors and wandered off. He had not been missing for more than 15 minutes. He looked at me as if to say, "Likely story," picked up my screaming son in a vice-grip, and threw him in the back of his patrol SUV. His boss came shortly – a blue-eyed Caucasian with a kind face. He came close to me and questioned me on what occurred. I explained my story. By then I was almost hysterical, as the first officer had already threatened to take my son away from me, and lock me up for neglect.

His supervisor said after he heard my story: "I have children, so I can certainly understand how something like this could occur. Just be careful and keep a close eye on him from now on." From that day forward, I was fearful of allowing my son out of my sight. I clung to him so tightly, as if I wouldn't let him go. Although that incident occurred over 5 years ago, he speaks about it occasionally as if it happened just yesterday.

The challenges seemed unending, and several times people would ask me if I would reconcile with my ex. Because everyone did not know all the details, they did not understand that we could not live together anymore. I felt that I preferred to struggle and "do bad by myself," than to revert to what I had experienced before. There were days when food was in short supply, but those days were not desperate days. If I ever felt too hungry, I could call my grandmother and stop by for a warm, tasty meal. Keeping up with rent and daycare on one income was very challenging. I was determined that even if I ended up in court, I was not accepting an eviction. I had nowhere to go - unless I was to return home to my dad. I even asked my father if I could move back home once, but I never followed through with it. Being on my own with no one to turn to was hard, but it was also good because it helped me to become disciplined, especially in my spending. I began to operate on a "cash only" basis while I cleared up consumer debt. After a while, I realized that I could live without using credit. I began viewing extended credit as "bad for me". Currently, my total debt is minimal in comparison to where I was just 5 years ago, and I have a new mortgage from my recently purchased home – owned only by me. When I look back at where I was financially to where I am today, I cannot help but lift my hands in praise daily to the God I serve!!!

Being single, even with a child, means I had some extra time on my hands to do some things to make life better for us. Within two months of my divorce, I began my online studies for a Master's degree in Business Administration, with a concentration in Global Management. It has been an arduous task, especially since I graduated from college 14 years ago. The coursework has been challenging but interesting. I learned new concepts such as how the U.S. Federal Government determines interest rates for consumer loans and what GDP (Gross Domestic Product) means. I've met some very interesting people during my online studies. I have learned how to write persuasively, as most of my papers require me to defend my positions with supporting evidence. I have also come to love the process of learning new concepts, which I plan to use as a springboard into the next phase of my career life. I am determined to graduate in 2012.

Another activity I became involved in was social networking. I was invited by my then-best friend to MySpace, where I found my writing voice. I published approximately 85 entries over a two and a-half year period and gained a following. The following astounded me because I intended to write only for myself, much like a journal. In those reflective pieces I began to gain wholeness and healing. I freely expressed anger and frustration, which eventually gave way to forgiveness and renewal. I learned how to love my ex in a different way, as I do not use the past for present debates anymore, and I try to see him as who he is today – a responsible father who is doing his best to provide for his son. I also realize that holding on to the past will hold me hostage to the past. I am determined to move on with my life and not dwell on those dark moments. I also learned how to gain his trust and respect by not belittling his efforts and by giving him the chance to be a better "him" without negativity. I can honestly say that we are friends today and work closely together as a team to raise our son.

I met and became friends with several interesting people on MySpace. One is the author of "Dark Blessing", Elder Lenore Artis. This extraordinary woman began stopping by my page to encourage me. When I learned that we lived in the same state, I knew it was only a matter of time before we would meet. I was elated to visit her church and to have her come out of her seat and give me the biggest bear hug ever! We have been friends ever since. I know that God has greater in store for her life. When people come alongside you to encourage you and give great advice – even when they have accomplished much more than you have – such individuals typically have your best interest at heart.

I was also invited by Linda Grosvenor to become a friend and to join her new website www.ThePluralThing.com. When I joined in December of 2007 I had NO IDEA the impact that her book: "The Plural Thing: Spiritually

| Single Again |

Preparing for Your Soul Mate" and website would have on my thought-life. The book and website are filled with insights on how to prepare for marriage, how to break soul ties and other relevant and interesting information and discussion threads. I did a lot of soul-searching and repenting because the dysfunction I experienced in my relationship also stemmed from my ignorance on how to be a good wife. Her site and book played the biggest roles in helping me heal from the emotional pain I was experiencing at that time. Linda and her husband Calvin are now friends of mine! I have also made new friends as a result of that divine connection. The site has been a tremendous blessing. I recommended it to many people. Look it up: www.ThePluralThing.com

"It Is Well With My Soul"

I have a strong spiritual heritage.

Previous generations in my family (on both sides) were entrenched in church. My dad was originally Baptist and became Pentecostal once he met my Mom. His older sisters are Seventh Day Adventist. My mom's family is a mixture of Pentecostal and Seventh Day Adventist.

Grandma told us that our mom accepted Jesus into her heart at the age of 11. Grandma had also accepted Christ on the same night; she was in her late 20's. My mother experienced the baptism of the Holy Spirit on that night of destiny, and moved with authority and passion from that moment until she departed this life. Grandma, Daddy and Mommy were Sunday School teachers. Grandma was also a literacy teacher for a government-sponsored "Second Chance" educational program for adults. Mommy was an evangelist (part time). She was invited to speak in various churches for Women's Day events.

My family is also musically inclined; once several family members offered a hymn selection (I don't recall the exact hymn title) at our church in NJ! This was shortly after Mommy departed this life. Grandma taught the youth choir before I was born; she played the piano and sang. Mommy taught us how to play the recorder. And Daddy has a FANTASTIC tenor voice!

I accepted Jesus into my heart at the age of 12, one Sunday, at our home church in Jamaica. Our senior pastor preached from the Book of Revelation, on the end times. He preached about what life may be like, on earth, for those who do not accept Jesus in their hearts, and are left behind to face the Great Tribulation. I was TERRIFIED when I heard this sermon. I decided I wanted to go to heaven and not get left behind.

I had heard about Jesus all my life; my family made sure of that. We had early-morning family devotions at 5am every Sunday. At the age of about 4 or 5 we were expected to join in and pray. We also took turns reading the Scriptures and/or praying aloud. We sang the old hymns of our faith. I know many hymns by heart because of those intimate moments spent before God with my family. One of my favorites to this day is "My Hope Is Built". I cannot forget "Trust & Obey" – our parents LOVED singing that one.

I was raised to believe that those who accept Jesus Christ as Savior and Lord of their lives should follow in His steps by participating in water baptism (by immersion), Holy Communion and foot washing. I was allowed to participate in Communion, but I was held back from water baptism and foot washing for sanitary reasons.

At the age of 17 I felt ready to follow Jesus' example and to become baptized. I was now in the U.S. and chlorination was adequate for the water in which I would be baptized. It was an exhilarating experience. My younger sister (the middle sibling) followed me in baptism on the same day. Then something phenomenal occurred: I received the baptism (or in-filling) of the Holy Spirit exactly one week after being water-baptized!

The night of our water baptism, we went back to the church to be added as new members. (Water baptism service was held at the local YMCA pool.) Our pastor preached about the need to be filled with the Holy Spirit, so we would be equipped to live the Christian life and to face daily challenges without wavering. He prayed for each of us who were baptized that night and several of us felt free to worship God like never before. I decided that week that the following Sunday would be my turn for an in-filling of the Holy Spirit, so all week long I prayed specifically for that gift. I fasted from one meal

"It Is Well With My Soul"

every day. On the following Sunday, I went to church with an air of anticipation and expectation. Sunday morning was a regular service, but on Sunday night, as I worshipped at the altar, a bright, blinding light shone over me. It was brighter than the lights in the church. My eyes were closed and my hands were upraised. The light was so bright that I felt like a flashlight was being shone in my eyes. Then my pastor anointed his hands with anointing oil and laid it on our lips (as several of us were at the altar). Immediately after he touched my lips I spoke in a different language, one I had never learned! I felt cleansed – like a brand new person! From that day forward, it became easier for me to pray and spend time with God.

However, by age 19, I felt angry about all the stresses and changes that were taking place all around me. I felt misunderstood and wondered if the God I prayed to even cared or was concerned about my daily struggles. My times of spiritual reflection began to wane in light of my personal doubts. I had even given up on attending church and was content to stay home and hibernate in my room. I was still living at home (when I was visiting from college) at that time. My dad made it clear: "Everyone living under this roof goes to church." Before I felt convinced in returning to church, I was invited to an event where a guest pastor preached. As he spoke about the experiences I was having (as he said, "You may feel misunderstood, and that no-one really cares about what you are going through"), he made me wonder if anyone told him about my personal struggles. I knew then that I was destined to hear that particular sermon on that evening. I felt that God wanted me back in the place I left behind, so I made up my mind to return to church and to become involved in helping our youth.

After resuming church attendance, I became very involved. I was a Praise Team member, and lead soloist on the church choir. When I was married I became the youth president (for 2 years) and the youth choir president (for 2 years after my youth president term ended). I LOVE youth! Their vibrancy and frankness keeps me thinking, praying and laughing HILARIOUSLY! I was able to motivate them to do things that they never thought they could do. For example, when I was the youth president we won the District Sports Day (also known as Field Day) for the first time ever!!! The celebration was intense! When I was the choir president we started touring and singing at other churches. We even had choir anniversaries. My last event was our 2002 anniversary. I retired from my post to deliver my son and never returned to that position.

As my marriage crumbled, I dug into the Scriptures. I spoke frequently with a close girlfriend who was also going through a rough marriage. We consoled each other and shared Scripture references to comfort us and keep us going. I fasted and prayed continually. I had warfare prayers by walking throughout my home on every level (from the basement to the second floor) while declaring the Word of God out loud over every circumstance. My spouse would look at me as if I was strange every time I did it, but I did not care. I was raised by my family to fight in the spirit, and I am continuing the spiritual legacy that was passed down to me and my child.

My discipleship journey continues to stretch me in various directions. At my current church, I was recently appointed as an Adult Sunday School teacher, and I have been a Praise and Worship Leader on the church choir for almost 2 years. One thing I can fully rely on is my faith. I sing about Jesus all day. I will sometimes pause and be reminded of a Scripture verse or passage I have committed to memory and repeat it to calm and comfort my mind and emotions.

My Christian faith is my foundation.

Miracles In Abundance

Throughout my life, I have personally witnessed and experienced many miracles. A few specific instances come to mind.

When I was about 11 I had a severe asthma attack. My attacks would come on so forcefully, that I could not sleep or eat. All of my energies would be focused on breathing. Attacks would last about 2 to 3 days, and were very exhausting. One weekend I was very sick. My mother kept vigil during the day, that Sunday, so my grandmother could go to church. When night came, my mother got dressed to go to night service. She left and said quietly that she was going to pray for me. I was too sick to care.

As I lay on the bed, struggling to breathe, suddenly my breathing spasms stopped! At first I did not notice it, but after a while, I sat up in bed and sat on the edge of the bed, enjoying lungfuls of air easily. My grandmother came in the room to check on me. I told her "I feel better!" She was cautious because it was so sudden. When Mommy got home, she told us that the pastor and the church went into serious prayer for me. When we checked the time we realized that my moment of healing and deliverance coincided with the time of those heartfelt prayers. I am now in my 30's, and I can testify that I have never had a severe asthma attack since that day! I thank God for healing my body!

Another instance comes to mind: I was trying to conceive in the marriage and I was not sure if it had occurred. I was scheduled for a mammogram, due to family history, so I went in the room, undressed and prepared to go in front of the machine. The lady looked at me kindly and said, "Is there any chance you may be pregnant?" I looked at her, a bit embarrassed, and thought for a few moments. I started doing a mental check and told her I was not sure. She said, "Why don't you reschedule after you confirm? Would you want this baby if you are pregnant?" I did not hesitate in my response, "Yes, of course!" So I got dressed and left the screening center. Within one week I purchased a couple pregnancy tests. And you guessed it: I was PREGNANT. I thank God for that lady, because I had no symptoms of pregnancy. If I had taken the mammogram there is no telling what could have happened to my son as he was very young, less than 1 month conceived. God protected him from the risk of deformity or death. Amen!

Grandma

My grandmother's strength had been failing for quite some time, but her fierce independence made it difficult to do more for her – until that fateful day, in June 2009, when she slipped and fell in her bathroom and laid on the floor all night in excruciating pain. She broke her hip; she was too far away from the call button in her bathroom so she had to lay there for several hours. Thankfully a health aide had begun coming in to help her, 2 weeks prior to the incident. When the aide knocked to come in, she told her to go and get help for her. The social services coordinator called to let me know of the issue. I dropped everything at work and ran out of my workplace to the hospital.

After a day of screening, testing and X-rays and such, they determined that only her hip was broken. Two days later, after urgent surgery, she was eased back into life. She began rehabilitation a few days after the surgery, so she would be able to walk again. After the committed efforts of the rehab professionals (she was in two rehab locations) she was able to walk with the aid of a walker. She returned to her apartment in Aug 2009, approximately 2 months after breaking her hip.

We began an intense coordination of efforts and personal schedules to keep her fed and bathed, and her clothing and apartment clean. She still spent nights alone because the rules of her senior apartment building did not allow individuals to stay every night unless they were caregivers. We did not have finances to pay anyone to do that. Four months later, at 3am in the morning, I received a call that she had fallen again. The emergency medical technicians showed up, but she refused to go to the hospital. They helped her back into bed. Later that morning, I called constantly to check on her status, but did not receive an answer. I discovered that she fell on the floor again and refused to press her personal emergency pendant for help. Since the paramedics had shown up the first time and she refused treatment, as she did not "want to be a bother to them." Grandma was taken and admitted to the hospital again. After a short stay she was sent to another nursing home, recommended by her power of attorney. Approximately 1 month after her stay in the nursing home, she started having trouble breathing. They treated her for asthma, but she still could not breathe. She fell ill; she had developed pneumonia for the first time in her life.

She stayed in the hospital for almost one month. Her recovery was slow and deliberate. She became despondent. Because of H1N1 flu restrictions, I was unable to take my son for visits, so I could not see her very often. After she recovered, she went back to the nursing home to regain her strength.

We had a huge progress meeting on Grandma's behalf at the nursing home. The conclusion of the meeting was to have her stay in the nursing home, for the time being, so that she could receive her daily medications. Work schedules prevented the family from being able to administer her medication at home and the exorbitant cost hindered us from hiring someone to do it. Keeping her where she was seemed the best option. I made the agonizing decision for her to stay at the nursing home and visit my home occasionally for a change of scenery. It is hard to do this without feeling guilty. I am still trying to reconcile this within myself, but it will take some time. I never, in one million years, thought my grandmother would be in a nursing home and not with me. She has contributed so much to our family; it just does not seem fair for her to end up this way.

Moving Forward

As my life continues, I anticipate brighter, better days.

Moments of overwhelming grief, disappointment, anxiety and frustration have played major roles in my life, but there are also moments of great memories and rewarding times. I enjoy moments spent with family members and treasured friends. Love has not left my side at all! I have mentors for every aspect of my life and praying people cover me and my son often.

God has been very good to me throughout all my life. Even in the midst of every struggle, He made a way out for me. Dark days have never lasted longer than I could handle. I am thankful for the loving relationship I have with my son, who is now almost as tall as I am. He has become my protector and enjoys the company of both parents. My son is brilliant, has a very pleasant personality, and he is a lot of fun to be around.

My relationship with John is much better than before. The painful memories are in the past, and I make every effort to focus heavily on the positive things and push the negatives into the background. Every person is a work in progress, and is growing and developing. Extending grace is necessary for maturity and for moving forward. I believe we will always be friends, especially for the sake of our son. Over the years I began setting boundaries for our conversations, so that I would be addressed always with respect. I used to say, "I might look the same, but I am not the same." I shared many times with him how he made me feel and how some of his angry rants affected our son, which I believe helped to bring change. I have also observed levels of growth and maturity in him with time. We still disagree on some issues, but they do not happen as often as before and we are able to resolve many of them, which is different from the past. I believe that prayer has also helped us to come together, because we have to raise our son and we needed to set an example for him to follow.

As I embrace my future in faith, I believe that everything God has promised me will come to pass. This includes a God-fearing, kind and loving husband and the blossoming of a ministry to encourage single young women and to support senior citizens.

Though the road has been rough, the struggles I endured truly helped me grow. Most importantly they helped me realize my own worth. When you go through trials, and find yourself in places you never thought you'd be, in a lot of ways, you begin to beat up on yourself. As I've said, I spent so much time being disappointed in myself and the decisions I made. I would sit and interrogate myself about why I didn't listen to my intuition, or why I didn't leave, but through all of that God remained by my side. He didn't waste time accusing me or judging me, He simply guided me, constantly helping me build a bridge from a place of misery to a place a victory. It was God's faithfulness to me that made me realize my worth. It reminds me of CeCe Winans song, Alabaster Box.

My Life: Ten Years Later

Recently I posted on social media a "How Much Have You Changed Challenge" side-by-side photo comparison that was fourteen years apart. The differences between both photos were remarkable. My first photo was taken in the same year of my divorce. My eyes looked blank and dazed. I was clearly unhappy. My second photo graces the front cover of this edition and was taken this year (2021). The joy is unmistakable, and I make no apologies for it.

Life has taken many twists and turns over the last ten years (in fact, it's eleven years, as the manuscript was originally penned in 2010). I know you may be wondering – so, how did Michelle and her son manage during these last ten years? What about her family – how are they?

Get ready, because A LOT has happened, and I am sharing a summary to bring you up to date on where we are now.

FIRST: I am still unmarried. I still desire to be married again, but it has not happened yet. At first it was troubling to me, but then I realized that I needed to focus on raising my son - and I did just that. I am calm, relaxed and content. It took a while for me to get to this point, but I am assured that nothing happens by accident or coincidence. I firmly hold on to what was promised to me years ago, and I believe that I am very close to meeting the man that God has for me. I continue to rest in that promise.

SCHOOL DAYS: I recall commentary from one of my high school friends who read the first edition of this book. She sent me a private message on social media to say how much she enjoyed my book, but how she regretted not stepping in to defend or comfort me during the years of turmoil in school. I acknowledged her comment, and I realized as well that I probably did not display most of my angst outwardly for everyone to see, so she probably did not know or realize how horrible things really were for me. The trauma of my school days is something that I am still working through today, as friendships with women has been challenging as a result. In my past, they could not be trusted. But.... God is doing a new thing in my life. He has brought me closer to my siblings, and I have been introduced to godly women who want to see me win. This is different, but a "good" different – if you understand what I mean. I am grateful for who He has sent my way.

JAMAICA: My island home will always be home for me, no matter where I live. I had the wonderful opportunity to visit a few times over the past ten years. My first time speaking to a large audience about *"It's My Life"* happened right there on the island! I will always be thankful for Duhaney Park New Testament Church of God's gracious pastor, Rev Christopher Hutchinson, for taking a chance on me one beautiful Sunday morning several years ago. We were all blessed and encouraged on that day. I prayed for some of the attendees as they worshipped and cried at the altar. I will never forget that day. I hope to visit them again very soon.

MY FAMILY: Everyone is doing well. Daddy and I have grown closer over the last ten years, and now he is one of my best friends. He has been my biggest supporter ever since the first edition of this book was released. He has attended every new book launch since then, and he shares my work with others. I am grateful that we still have him with us. He is still very active, and I think he's still busier than I am! He has celebrated many wedding anniversaries with his second wife.

My sisters and I got closer in an unusual way via the pandemic of 2020. We first connected out of concern for each other's wellbeing, and then it developed into something much more. We are three parts of one woman who we lost over thirty years ago, and we have realized that together we are a powerful force to be reckoned with. We started a podcast that has encouraged and uplifted us, and now has several faithful listeners. "SeedPlanters with the Cameron Family" can be heard on every major podcast platform. We got Daddy to join in on some of our sessions too! You can take a listen and let us know what you think!

You may be wondering about Grandma. She left us shortly after a significant downturn in her health in 2013. She was 89. We miss her so much, as she was like our second mother.

And my son? He is six feet tall! He is quite handsome, and he's now a young man who is ready to take on the world. High school was challenging especially in terms of his health, but my heart burst with pride as he walked up to receive his high school diploma. What appeared to be impossible, God made it VERY possible! We are still rejoicing today.

BOOKS: I have written several books over the past ten years. My books target readers who are single and who are interested in writing and publishing books. After I published a couple books, people started to ask me to explain the process – so I started hosting writing workshops in 2019. So far, I have worked with several authors, some of whom have written and published multiple books; some are bestsellers. I started editing for clients in 2015 when one of my internet friends sent a manuscript to me to lighten her workload. Since then, I have lost count of the number of books that have crossed my path for editing. With returning editing clients and referrals, I am rarely without editing work. The joy and depth that these authors have brought into my life – I don't think they realize how privileged I feel to have played a role in their writing and publishing journeys!

SPEAKING: I decided this summer (2021) to hone and develop my speaking career some more. Thanks to Shawn Fair and the Fair Consulting Group, I was extended a special opportunity and I am excited to stand on a prominent stage this month (September 2021) to share a snippet of my story and to offer my assistance to those who want to tell their stories too. I look forward to the outcome of that event!

SINGLES: Because I understood the journey of singleness and I kept meeting singles who were just existing vs truly living, in 2016 I co-launched a singles ministry in New Jersey that is not affiliated with any church denomination. With oversight from Overseer Christopher Jones, we have hosted some amazing events and life-changing moments over the years. Popular speakers were invited to present to the attendees (from the Tristate area and beyond), and strong connections were made. It is my hope and desire to continue to host events again soon when possible.

CHALLENGES: I have experienced several challenging moments over the past ten years. With employment changes and health challenges, I had to make significant decisions. Thankfully I am now on the right path, and my health is closer to where I want it to be. Sometimes we hold on to scenarios that we think we must have, until we realize that we can thrive without them. The peace of mind and wholeness cannot be discounted once you let go of what no longer serves you.

WHAT'S NEXT? Good question! Your guess is as good as mine. As life continues to unfold, I look forward to each new opportunity and every new connection. I am embracing every moment as I am grateful to be alive and well to enjoy what is happening and what will happen. I will celebrate a milestone birthday in 2022. I am EXCITED!

Thank you for journeying with me!

My contact information is on the last page of this book, so do not hesitate to reach out and connect!

Reflective Prose Pieces from My Life

Based on the requests of many of my readers over the years, I decided to add this section to my autobiography. This is a compilation of reflective pieces I wrote and posted on MySpace and Facebook over a 4 year span; they are listed randomly. Various experiences are reflected in each, with lessons learned. These are my life-lessons and memoirs. Reflect and enjoy.

Your Net Worth

"You don't know the cost of the oil in my alabaster box."
(CeCe Winans, The Alabaster Box)

Do you know the cost of your oil?

This song ministers to me every time I hear it. You see, in Biblical times, oil was considered a precious commodity and used in many facets of life. As such, in those days, one's wealth was partially based on that individual's capacity to produce pure oil. And so it was then, so it is today. During my lowest times I was not placing enough emphasis and value on the wonderful gifts God had given me - my spirit, soul and body. I'd venture to say that I am not alone. What value do you place on your spirit, soul and body? What is your net worth?

We live in a world where net worth is determined by what someone drives, who they know (or who knows them), where they live or where they work. But what about character? Questions like: Can you be trusted if all the lights go out and no-one is around? or What happens if you lose the fancy car, the luxurious house and the "friends" that came with the car and the house, are the aspects of a person's life that really matter.

I've learned to look beyond the fluff, and I have come to realize that it isn't what I own (or what owns me) or who I know, but my real worth is realized by Who knows me. Yes, God knows me and has valued me and you so highly that He sent His only Son, Jesus the Christ, to live here on the earth, to walk and talk with humans, and to feel hunger, pain and rejection just like any of us. Some of us are popular and can draw a crowd of adoring fans anywhere, anytime. Many of us are average people making the best of our situations. The key is our foundation. Through the various obstacles in my life, God has become so firmly rooted in my foundation that I can't make a move without Him. He carries me though every situation.

I know that there are many of us who believe that life is as a result of an accident – the Big Bang. This thought pattern allows many of us not to care too much about how we conduct our lives on a daily basis. Even some of us who claim to know God may conduct our lives with little caution. But life has taught me that we shouldn't be so easily accessible. We shouldn't just let ANYBODY sleep in our beds or get that close to us. After all, we are prizes of great value as demonstrated by Christ's sacrifice for us. This value should follow us in all aspects of our lives – the things we eat, even the things we think about.

I used to see myself based on what I thought others were attracted to – the "loud" people, who always had something witty to say, which caused uproarious laughter, those with all the money they could ever want, so "drinks were (always) on the house". Since I did not fit into any of these categories, I felt "less than" others. But with time spent in the Word of God, and after experiencing some very sensitive situations, I am healing inside and I now view my net worth as more than just monetary value, or the ability to draw a crowd. I am VERY valuable to my Maker, Sustainer and Savior. My oil is worth more than anyone could ever pay for it, because it was first purchased with the life and blood of a mighty, Holy God's Son. That is something I can't even redeem. The only thing left for me to do is cherish what God has placed inside of me. So, because of that precious oil I dare to dream again of love that will last until one of us dies. I dare to dream of financial success regardless of what the economists and financial analysts say. I dare to dream of career fulfillment as I battle with difficult academic classes.

| *Your Net Worth* |

What is your net worth? Do you know? Does it matter to you? Remember, you were redeemed with a high price.

Protect your value. Guard your wellspring. Cherish your oil.

1 Corinthians 6: 20 (KJV) *"For ye are bought with a price: therefore glorify God in your body, and in your spirit, which are God's."*

Personal Introspection

Over the years, as my marriage disintegrated, I began the process of intense introspection. Although several years have passed since my divorce, I discovered that this is a never-ending journey. I have always been a thinker from a young age, but in recent years I have discovered a wellspring deep within that was untapped for many years.

Learning about you is the one thing that everyone should strive to do. It helps to know who you are. If we do not know ourselves, how can anyone else know who we are? Certainly most of us would state "I know who I am!" but we would be surprised to know how little we really do know about ourselves. My depressing and unexpected marital situation caused me to learn a few things about myself.

One of the realizations I have come to is that I MUST be in an emotionally healthy environment. I cannot live with continuous strife and anger all around me. Peace and quiet (unless it is pleasant noise such as laughter or playing) must be primary. Yelling, cursing, rage and all that comes with the territory actually terrifies me.

I also realize I have to learn to trust again so I can love again. This does not only apply to men; I find that I am also very wary of women. I have had several best friends over the years, but I have found that after a while I was being used, lied to or being manipulated in some way so I had to step back. Life has caused me to wonder aloud who is really real. When I see certain behaviors, I may compare them to past experiences to see if I've seen this before. Still these things cannot keep me in bondage. I have to learn to trust again and not hold the misdeeds of people in my past against the people of my present.

Additionally, I am analytical by nature, so I have learned that some things need less thought and analysis and more action. I discovered that I can talk myself into and out of almost anything. This might make me seem as if I don't know what I want. Sometimes I do not, but many times I do and yet I find reasons to say to myself "That is not for YOU."

> *Fear can swallow me up if I allow it. As a shy, quiet woman I have never purposely sought the forefront in anything, but my gifts and abilities have made room for me. As a result, I have no choice but to allow what is within me to come out. For example, the task of writing this book cannot be underestimated. I know that writing about my intimate moments in life will open my personal story up to people whom I may never meet. Although I may have been tempted to put this manuscript aside and pursue something else, several of my coaches pushed me and encouraged me to keep on writing.*

I can be stubborn, but I try to be that way for the right reasons. I refuse to lie down and give up on life. I have experienced many set backs, but I am determined to get past them and allow the struggle to become tools for growth and development. I am aware that emotional scars can mark our souls for a lifetime, but I am determined to win this war that has been waging within my heart.

Finally, one of my new mantras is - I will leave you in God's hands. This means that if someone is mistreating me, I will not take it upon myself to vindicate or fight for my rights. I will do what is necessary to protect my interests but I will not act in vengeance. I learned that we reap whatever we sow. I want to reap good and not evil so I cannot do evil to someone just because they hurt me.

| *Personal Introspection* |

My love for God is my true foundation. Without my relationship with Jesus Christ I believe my mind would have been shattered many years ago. I also value character and integrity more than anything else. I love to be around those who are visually appealing, but if he or she is dishonest or lives a double life, I must move on.

Truth - Today's Precious Commodity

Today's news is filled with those who were once trusted, who we now know were scammers and schemers from the outset (or fell by the wayside over time). My heart gets heavy when the news reveals leaders in the body of Christ whom many have supported, prayed for and aligned themselves with in the past performing acts of lewdness, violence or wreaking financial havoc when no one is looking.

When I read the Bible, I see many references where God desires that our hearts' motives be pure and intentional and drive what we do and/or say. In **Deuteronomy 25:15 (NIV)** God declared to the Israelites: *"You must have accurate and honest weights and measures, so that you may live long in the land the LORD your God is giving you."*

King David prays to God as they receive gifts from the nation of Israel to build the temple (the one that King Solomon, his son, built):

"I know, my God, that you test the heart and are pleased with integrity. All these things have I given willingly and with honest intent. And now I have seen with joy how willingly your people who are here have given to you." (I **Chronicles 29:17**)

Proverbs 24:26 states *"An honest answer is like a kiss on the lips."*

I also just discovered an interesting phenomenon: Jesus prefaced many of his teachings with "I tell you the truth" (see www.biblegateway.com, search "truth", NIV version). With countless other references to truth, integrity and honesty in the Scriptures, I am positive that God places a high premium on all three character traits.

On Dictionary.com, truth is defined as "the true or actual state of a matter." Integrity is stated as "adherence to moral and ethical principles; soundness of moral character; honesty." Honesty is "truthfulness, sincerity, or frankness."

With the increase of personalized technology, more opportunities to cover, hide and create an alternate personality are available. Marriages are crumbling at an alarming rate, as private networking occurs on cell phones and computers. We can say one thing to one person and say something totally different to another person, with no thought of why we do not state the truth clearly, wherever we are, no matter whom we are with.

I believe that fear of rejection is one of the main reasons we sometimes find it easier to lie, or bend the truth or act dishonestly. Many of us truly desire the companionship/friendships/accolades of peers (socially) and top management within our companies. We want to impress them, even when it is not genuine. The shame comes later when our falsehood is discovered and the rejection we tried so hard to avoid becomes a self-fulfilling prophecy.

I strongly believe that if we do not take too much stock in what other people think or believe about us, and instead place more focus on what is written in the Word of God, our obedience to His Word will provide the blessings that we desire. Taking matters into our own hands and attempting to "fix the fight," so we come out on top, always yields disastrous results. When we are willing to speak the truth, even if it costs us our jobs, or alienates us from people we desire to be close to, then that is a worthwhile risk to take. Why? Because the final outcome reaps benefits we cannot duplicate or create ourselves. I remember having a difficult time at work with a manager who tried to paint a bad picture of my performance and my ability to work with others. I was interviewed by Human Resources and upper management and told them my side of the story. In the end, without my interference or manipulation, my work situation was changed radically and my manager was let go. This was a situation that I had no control over. I just had to sit back and allow God to fight on my behalf.

Take King David, for example (read 2 Samuel chapters 11 & 12). David is known as the king who should have been out to war in the spring one year, with all the other soldiers. Instead he stayed home, spied a beautiful woman bathing and things went downhill pretty fast from that moment onward. He created layers of dishonesty and tried to cover one sinful act with another, until Nathan, the prophet, boldly came into his presence and unveiled the "situation." The reason King David is such a fantastic example is that he didn't perpetuate the mess once he was confronted; he repented. He surrendered his sordid affair/murder situation into God's hands, and his life was spared and his kingdom remained intact. He was called "a man after my own heart" by God Himself. In his imperfect state (which is the same for all of us) he recognized his shortcomings, owned up to them and became real and transparent. He was part of that rare breed.

Many of us admire those who dare to stand apart from the crowd and unveil their hearts to the world. We secretly wish we could be as bold or as open as they are. But I have come to realize what remains in secret, keeps you in bondage! Once it comes out and it is handled appropriately (you may need to seek professional guidance or assistance with some issues) you are free to be the person you were meant to be! Your "real you" can now step forward and take his/her rightful place in society and in ministry! When my marriage was ending, several people in the church I was attending, and who knew we were in trouble, begged me to stay because of what others would think if I left. I told them it made no sense for me to stay just because of what others may say if I moved out. I felt that censoring my life because of others' opinion meant I would live in bondage forever, pretending to enjoy something that was destroying me inside.

I had to be willing to take my mask off. Many of us are walking around, working, living and worshipping via our alter ego. Many of us have never met the real "you." It took great effort, but my designated representative had to be removed! She shows up again from time to time, but I fight back by allowing God's Spirit to come in and remove that tendency to wander away from His truths. His promises to bless us are not unreal; King David is a testimony to that fact! I also stand as a witness, because God did it for me!

And He can do it for YOU too!!! Let's put on our belt of truth today (Ephesians 6:14) so we can continue to fight and win life's battles together. Will you join me???

So What's Normal, Anyhow?

(posted on www.lovebettercamp.com on April 21, 2008)

One of the greatest things that bind us in this world is comparison and this false notion of normalcy. I recently discovered that what I viewed as "normal" doesn't really exist.

I was raised in a conservative Christian household, and as a shy, overweight girl, I sought to be accepted among my peers. It was tough. I was teased daily, and I cried daily. As this trend continued into my teen years I developed a new strategy - I'd become "tough". I think the trauma of growing up feeling as if I didn't meet the bar and that I was always "on the outside looking in," caused me to think that I did not really deserve better than what I had or what I'd previously experienced. These feelings also caused me to allow people to use me.

I married and divorced within a ten-year span, again because I thought I was fortunate to have such an attractive man who had physique and charm. I paid no attention to fact that he was not fulfilling what I needed in a relationship. It was rocky, verbally abusive and mentally crushing. It wasn't until I believed I was worthy of a better situation that I was willing or able to climb out of that damaging relationship.

What I failed to see was all the value and potential God saw in me. For as long as I can remember, I was the consummate people pleaser. I've never wanted to hurt feelings, but now I have a deeper desire to understand what

God may be saying vs. what I or others may say, think or believe. I desire to do what He wants. The change is gradual, but I believe it is visible. Now that I am on the road of recovery, I've also dropped some draining "friendships". I've made a pledge to myself - every time I want to make a commitment to someone or agree to something, I must ask myself "WHY???" Is it because I'm settling AGAIN for what I consider "normal" or am I trying to please others? Or does it really reflect the God that I serve and what I should accept, because of my relationship with Him? This does not mean I'm not humble or meek, but it means I will not think of myself as less than someone else. I no longer think I don't deserve better treatment or a better situation. Instead I view myself (daily) with dignity and as one who is made in the image of God.

I am bought with a price, which is the blood of Jesus Christ. I am an heir and joint-heir with Jesus. I am special to Him and I belong to the body of Christ. My life matters to Him. My situations matter. My relationships matter. My personal issues matter to Him, and that makes me and my situations important.

Normal. I am learning to accept that normal is an illusion, but who I am in Jesus Christ is the truth! **1 Corinthians 6:20 (KJV)** *"For ye are bought with a price: therefore glorify God in your body, and in your spirit, which are God's."*

Superficiality in Relationships

Recently I bought a nectarine which was flawless on the surface. I washed and prepared to eat it. When I bit into it I was shocked. The inside was mushy and smelled old. Of course I had to get rid of it because it was not fit for consumption.

This reminded me of superficiality in relationships.

Superficiality abounds in many of our everyday decisions. Choosing a marriage or relationship partner is no exception.

Dictionary.com defines "superficial" as:

1. concerned with or comprehending only what is on the surface or obvious: a superficial observer.
2. shallow; not profound or thorough: a superficial writer.
3. apparent rather than real.
4. insubstantial or insignificant: superficial improvements.

We tend to be attracted to a fantastic physique/figure, a nice voice, flashy/trendy clothing and autos – but after we dig beneath the surface, is anything there that is worthwhile?

| **It's My Life** *and I Live Here* |

It has been said that men are mostly visual beings, where they are attracted to a woman's outer beauty before they investigate to see if there is more to her than meets the eye. I must admit that I am also a visual lady and that a stacked physique and handsome features grab my attention immediately. Because of life's experiences I am learning to move beyond the visible and dig deeper. After all, living with a handsome dude who does not respect me, makes him not so handsome to me after a while.

What if we decided always to look beyond what we could see immediately? What if we decide not to let our minds wander just because we see a curvaceous woman or a "six-pack" man and realize that the exterior only covers what is inside? The true person is inside the "house" they were blessed to have. Being cute/handsome and not surrendered to the Lordship of Jesus Christ is a disaster waiting to happen. But oh, how absolutely fantastic it is when two people are attracted to each other's spirits! Their love lights up the room. We may even find ourselves asking "What does she see in him, anyway??" "She is not that attractive. I wouldn't be with her if I were him." Those couples have looked beyond what is on the surface and have dug deeper to mine the diamonds buried deep within that person.

I was involved in a vibrant young adult ministry and we had a discussion about what men consider in "wife material". The young men who attended had a chance to present their perspectives. It was interesting to hear that they are not really attracted to women who focus all their energy on attracting men by showing all her physical assets for the world to see. Women (wife material) who catch and hold their attention are those who are modest and have a mysterious air about them. Good men are intrigued by what is deep within and an interested man will pursue to find out what is happening on the inside!

| *Surperficiliaty in Relationships* |

Let us all determine within ourselves to go beyond the superficial and get to the heart of the matter. What may seem ordinary on the surface may be a gold mine waiting to be discovered!

Psalm 139: 1 – 3 *"O LORD, you have searched me and you know me. You know when I sit and when I rise; you perceive my thoughts from afar. You discern my going out and my lying down; you are familiar with all my ways."*

The Split

As I have grown and become more discerning, I have split up with several people over the years, and not just in romantic terms. Splitting up, calling it quits, walking away - whatever you call it - has become necessary for me to get to my destiny – for me to realize that potential I am pregnant with. The pain is there, the memories linger, the conversations are rehearsed in my mind, but I know I must move forward; no turning back. Turning back means going back to situations that once detained me, distracted me and degraded me. Turning back means going back to situations that I felt comfortable with, but they were not helping me. Turning back means hesitating about moving forward.

(Read Philippians 3 verses 13 & 14, NIV)

Some of you may have heard of the song that begins "Pregnant, possibilities, now birthed anew..." That song has been ringing in my head for some time now. In fact I need to pull out my CD and listen carefully to the words again. Notice the first line. It said Pregnant with possibilities. The possibilities represent what CAN BE, something that can happen in the future. Pregnancies, although they may happen frequently, do not always end up as healthy, live births. If that is the case in the natural realm, then so it is in the spirit realm.

We are all pregnant with possibility. But sometimes we aren't ready for what it takes to bring that potential to life. I know for the longest time I wasn't, in fact, I didn't even believe I was pregnant. But when I realized the life, the possibilities, the potential that was dying to be birthed inside of me, I knew I had to press forward in my journey. I had to do what it took to bring my all that was inside of me to life. So with tears in my eyes and pain in my heart, I press forward. With memories of good times and bad times, I press forward. With pressure, determination and destiny just ahead, I press forward. I refuse to be detained anymore. I refuse to be sucked dry by others' lives, intentions, lies and distractions.

The split will bring about another union - a stronger, bolder union with God, through His blessed Son, Jesus Christ. I am joined to Him, walking closer to Him and sensing His loving arms encircled around my heart.
The split is difficult, but easy. Painful, but filled with relief. Tearful, but bursting with laughter.

I must split, because I must hear: 'Well done, good and faithful servant! You have been faithful with a few things; I will put you in charge of many things. Come and share your master's happiness!' (Matthew 25 verse 21, NIV) I crave your prayers.

Death by Comparisons

Many of the decisions we make in our lives are based on comparisons. We want to be perceived in a certain way by others (whether we know them or not), so we make every effort to have the 'right' look (clothing, hair, etc.), drive the 'right' car, work for the 'right' company, be seen with the 'right' people and make sure we listen to every word that the 'right' guru of whatever we're interested in has to say. For me, it was my wish to be like someone else, especially like others who were considered beautiful, articulate or popular in some way. I would feel ashamed when I could not dress like them, or command attention like they could. I stayed away from many social events because I felt awkward and ugly.

This is not limited to those who aren't professing to be Christians, however. This illness has spread (or carried over) into the Salvation Camp, as we must be in attendance at the 'right' conference or be a member of the 'right' Christian organization or congregation; we begin to talk like, walk like, dress like or act like our favorite preacher or singer or whoever is the 'star' in our lives.

Then there are those of us who are more likely to compare ourselves to those around us – many times using our gifts, our talents or our positions (or all three!) to make others feel inadequate or feel as if they are not as spiritual, or not quite 'on our level'.

2 Corinthians chapter 10 verse 12 (New International Version) states: *"We do not dare to classify or compare ourselves with some who commend themselves. When they measure themselves by themselves and compare* *themselves with themselves, they are not wise."*

There is also a story in the Bible, James chapter 2 verses 1 to 7, that speaks out against favoring some more highly than others because of appearance. (Read it when you have a chance.)

Because we compare and we have our favorites, we may miss out on what God wants us to experience and understand. I have learned a few things in life:

*1. **Get to know and love yourself first.** God loves you just as you are RIGHT NOW. He's not waiting for you to become a better person before He will decide to love you. He loves you IN SPITE of who you are right now. Let that resonate within your spirit. Meditate on it! This simple truth will allow you to hold your head up with dignity and confidence, knowing that no-one has the right to make you feel inferior. And once you realize that someone is beginning to look down on you, deal with the issue and/or remove yourself from the situation.*

*2. **Understand that you are unique.** In my primary school (known as elementary school here in the USA), while growing up in Jamaica, we learned this word as a mantra: The teacher asked – "What is UNIQUE?" And we would respond by yelling: "UNIQUE! The only one of its kind!" So, comparisons are useless in many cases, because we are as unique as our fingerprints. (Did you know that even identical twins have unique fingerprints?)*

*3. **Know your life's purpose.** Many times we follow others and compare ourselves to others because we do not know or understand our life's purpose. Ask the Lord to show you where you fit in into God's Body here on earth. No two people have the exact same assignment. Each of us is meant to reach a certain group or sector of society – whether it's in our local communities or in other regions of the world. I may look at my friends' lives and the direction(s) they are taking and wistfully compare myself to them. In turn, they may look at my life and wonder -WHY did she ever make that decision? I'd NEVER do that! But we must realize that our life experiences and decision-making will all work together to prepare us for the ministry/ministries we have ahead of us. For example, when I listen to certain ministers' testimonies and I observe where they are in ministry right now, I can plainly see how their experiences have given them the authority to minister in the way they do today.*

*4. **Never ignore (or pre-judge) someone, no matter what your initial opinion of the individual may be.** Give them a chance to prove themselves to you FIRST. Ask the Holy Spirit to reveal the intentions of those around you. He can do that.*

5. Always remember that your heroes and mentors are fallible and have their own opinions or motives for the things they say or do. What that means is you may compare yourself to someone you admire and may want to get close to them and/or emulate the individual, but they may also have issues of the mind or heart of which you may not be aware; then once their skeletons are revealed you may be very disappointed or hurt.

6. Realize that the only way to gain the victory over the tendency to make comparisons is by applying the shed blood of Jesus Christ. Allow Him to speak to your spirit and to show you where you may be going wrong in that area of your life. I've fallen into that trap so many times, it's ridiculous. It's interesting that I should be writing about something with which I struggle so much, but I think this is God's way to help me work through it to gain real deliverance.

May we allow God to deliver us from the sin of comparisons.

Growing Pains - Introspection

(2009)

I am noticing a few things: Time seems to be speeding up at an alarming rate. As the days fly by I feel a growing sense of uneasiness/restlessness, which indicates that a seismic shift is about to take place in my life!

For the past few years I have been transitioning in many ways. Externally there are visible changes (I should do before and after pictures to really illustrate my point), but more importantly, there is an entire transformation in progress internally. I will attempt to summarize what stepping into my purpose looks like for me:

> **1. I am less likely to ask others for advice FIRST.**
> Not too long ago I would be on the phone placing all my life's decisions (in gory detail) on the table for others to review or critique; it was as if I didn't know ANYTHING for myself or about myself. What were my opinions on matters that would affect me most? What about asking God's guidance in situations? Because I did this all the time, others were able to mold me into what THEY wanted me to be vs. who God wants me to be. So, back to my first point: When I discovered that I was being manipulated by several close ties, I had to sever them. This meant I also had to step up and take responsibility for WHO I AM BECOMING. I had to say "Yes" and "No" to the hard questions. No longer do I need to lean heavily on others' spin on my situation. Who knows me better than me??? GOD, of course, but aside from Him, the obvious answer is ME. Then I also realized that not everyone who appears to be on your side is genuinely fighting on your team. Some would want nothing better than to derail my dreams and my destiny because it would make them look bigger and better if I fail. So, I am seeking less advice from others, and I am choosing more introspection and prayer instead.

2. I am now learning to face the results of my actions.
If I do what's right, or wrong, there are outcomes for each type of action. Instead of running from my teachable moments, I am learning to glean important lessons. I am also learning to celebrate my positive or right actions; it is difficult for me to celebrate "wins" because usually I am prepping for the next step.

3. I am realizing that my destiny belongs to ME and to MY FUTURE GENERATIONS.
My son is now six; he is my only child. I pray that what I plant will be the right type of crops that he will reap; I desire that my example will guide him in his childhood. I pray he knows how to make good decisions and how to allow God to take first place in his life. I pray that what I believe, know and experience will help to shape the lives of my future generations in positive ways.

4. I respect and defer to those who have more experience in life matters. I always carry a writing tablet and a pen with me. I will whip it out on occasion to scribe wise words being imparted to me directly, or should I happen to be within earshot of great advice or a memorable quote. Sitting under great leadership (such as at church) is a very wonderful experience for me. I LOVE to inhale wisdom and knowledge. But hearing (or writing down) the information is only the beginning. What I do with it matters MUCH more. My newest practice is to make every effort to place all I learned into practice and build on it, much like stepping stones.

This list could go on infinitely, but summarily I realize that growth is taking place in the important areas of my life. I desire to be ready for my breakthrough. Without adequate preparation I won't be able to walk into my God-ordained destiny.

I know, without a doubt, that "life unusual" is just around the corner!!!!

Grieving Loss

After my divorce I attended a very spiritual and celebratory wedding. As I watched the obvious joy radiating from the bride and groom's faces, knowing that they had both abstained from intimacy intentionally until that day, I knew they were in anticipation of what would happen after the celebrations ended.

When the minister said, "You may kiss the bride" I thought her new husband had just stopped at an oasis in a desert!!! As we screamed their names and clapped in excitement, a part of me twinged inside.

Jealous, you may think.

No.

I was SAD.

I was ANGRY.

I felt CHEATED.

The next morning, after the wonderful wedding and reception, I awoke with tears streaming down my face. I called myself "stupid" because I didn't see the signs that my ex had been unfaithful throughout our entire "courtship" and engagement. When I relived our wedding night, I became thoroughly disgusted with myself. If he had been waiting for me like I had waited for him, he would have pounced on me the moment we were alone! Instead, I waited, and waited and waited - until I had to take what rightfully belonged to me! Can you believe a woman approaching a man for intimacy on her WEDDING NIGHT????

I was a virgin on my wedding night. The real deal. At first I think my ex thought I was kidding, but when he realized that initial intimacy between us was not smooth sailing he knew I was telling the truth.

I had many misgivings before we became engaged and even up to one month prior to our wedding but I allowed the time I had invested in the relationship (of four years) and pressure from both families to dictate the outcome, which ended up as an unhealthy marriage.

While trying to "make do" with the relationship I chose, I lost time and gained pain. My self-esteem was brought down to new lows....

This is graphic and very personal, but I share this to make a few points.

1. Allow God to choose your marriage partner. Do NOT get in the way.

2. Allow Him to guide your thoughts and feelings regarding a prospect. Do NOT let others get in the way of that revelation.

3. Then, once you are in a relationship with who seems to be "the One", allow God to take full charge of your emotions and actions. Waiting for God to provide what belongs to you, all the way up to the altar, is the BEST way.

While I grieved over my loss as I watched my friends get married, God gently leaned over from the portals of heaven and placed this Scripture before me: **Ephesians 2: 1 - 10 (NIV):**
1As for you, you were dead in your transgressions and sins, 2in which you used to live when you followed the ways of this world and of the ruler of the kingdom of the air, the spirit who is now at work in those who are disobedient. 3All of

us also lived among them at one time, gratifying the cravings of our sinful nature[a] and following its desires and thoughts. Like the rest, we were by nature objects of wrath. 4But because of his great love for us, God, who is rich in mercy, 5made us alive with Christ even when we were dead in transgressions—it is by grace you have been saved. 6And God raised us up with Christ and seated us with him in the heavenly realms in Christ Jesus, 7in order that in the coming ages he might show the incomparable riches of his grace, expressed in his kindness to us in Christ Jesus. 8For it is by grace you have been saved, through faith—and this not from yourselves, it is the gift of God— 9not by works, so that no one can boast. 10For we are God's workmanship, created in Christ Jesus to do good works, which God prepared in advance for us to do.*

What I gathered from this revelatory Scripture is that I was walking according to the world's standards when I chose my first husband - the looks, the humorous personality, etc. God is merciful, so He's allowing me a second chance, just like he did for my friends. You see, although this is the first marriage for both of them, it was not their first serious relationship. They had also experienced heartache and pain. The joyful enthusiasm in how they approached their relationship was infectious. We (singles) respected them and looked to them as positive role models.

As I currently grieve my profound loss, I also understand that God has really wonderful plans for me just ahead.

My story hasn't ended with my failed relationship; my story is just beginning!!!!

All Things Are Possible - Just Believe!

(May 26, 2008)

You may desire lifelong companionship with a godly person, just as you have observed in others' lives - but do you believe that God can do that for YOU too, or are you settling for less?

How many of you know that what you believe in your heart works as a magnet to draw certain types of individuals to you? If you believe marriage cannot work because there aren't any good people left in the world, then guess who will come knocking every time? If you believe you are undeserving of a healthy, godly person for you to spend the rest of your life with, then how will they come?

Some of my friends and relatives who are single (who were once married or previously involved in other relationships) have written off ever being happy in a wonderful marriage. At first I thought that way too, but as time passed and as I read the Word of God continually, I am happy to say that my mindset has changed tremendously.

First, God stated clearly that *"He who finds a wife finds what is good and receives favor from the LORD."* **(Proverbs 18:22, NIV).** This means that God sanctions marriage and has already blessed it and called it good. His favor is on it, so marriage cannot be all bad!

What has given marriage a really bad rap is the involvement of two people who are not ready for marriage, or who are unequally yoked (such as a believer who is married to someone who is not a believer). Once both people are emotionally and spiritually healthy and WHOLE, and are equally yoked, God will bless that union in ways that were unimaginable in the past.

I am now paying special attention to all the relationships within my life, and I am setting them in order, so they do not have the chance to disrupt what God is about to place in my life. Friendships are wonderful and family is great, but they must have their set place in our lives; boundaries must be put in place. I am now very careful regarding the conversations I keep with anyone - married or single, male or female - as the mindset and attitude of others can influence my decisions and my mindset, whether I want to believe that or not. Surrounding myself with those who desire to have meaningful relationships with God and others is where I am now focused. If my personal atmosphere (my mindset, my attitude and the friends I keep) is made right, then I have every reason to expect the right man to step forward in God's timing.

Having bad experiences in the past does not guarantee bad experiences in the future - unless that is what you believe. I recall attending a bible study class sometime ago and the teacher asked "How many of you pray and make special requests to God?" Everyone raised their hands. He then asked "How many of you expect an answer when you pray?"

Only a few hands went up. Mine was one of them. Why spend time praying if you do not believe that what you pray for can actually happen? Is that a waste of time or what?

"Therefore I tell you, whatever you ask for in prayer, believe that you have received it, and it will be yours." **(Mark 11:24, NIV)**

"If you believe, you will receive whatever you ask for in prayer." **(Matthew 21:22, NIV)**

So, for all those who have written off the possibility of ever having a wonderful, godly marriage, understand that God has already endorsed such,

and is waiting for you to believe Him enough to provide it for you!
Why not dare to believe that God has someone special waiting in the wings, whom He is preparing to love and care about you as much as you desire? Why not believe someone is there who has no plans to destroy your life or to take advantage of you - only to add to you and to make things better for you?

I DARE YOU TO BELIEVE!!! All things are possible WITH GOD!

Can You Forgive?

(May 26, 2008)

Can you forgive?

I had the pleasure of listening to a prominent speaker recently discuss forgiveness, as she shared examples from her own life. As she spoke, thoughts of past and present situations that seemed unfair to me started parading across my mind. Things I had forgotten about knocked on the door of my heart and caused me to reflect.

I had been the type to look at others over the top rim of my glasses – until my life situations changed. Now I am the one that others are looking at in very strange ways. Having to forgive others, who caused grief and pain, and then realizing that I was also a source of grief and pain to others, is not easy to handle from either perspective. I tend to store up my feelings and eventually hide them – which I know is not very good. As I practice sharing my heart with others via writing, I find it is now easier to express my deepest thoughts and reflections even while speaking. Vocalizing (or reading) what you have always thought is indeed a healing balm.

Jesus, I surrender my pain, my disappointments, any misunderstandings and my resentment of situations from my past (and my present) into your hands. You knew me before I was formed in my mother's womb. You have purged my heart with your precious blood before; wash it clean once more. As I open my life before you and others, may souls be refreshed and may those who were once bound in spirit be loosed and set free to go forth and live out their purpose that You have preordained from the beginning of time.

    Forgive me of the hurts I have caused. Allow me to let go of those who hurt me, intentionally or not. Help me to have the heart to say, like Jesus did: "Father, forgive them, for they do not know what they are doing." (Luke 23:34, NIV)

The Covenant

Today, (one Saturday in July 2009) as I prepared to take my son out for an afternoon of fun and relaxation (unheard of in my vocabulary), I took up the Bible to read a portion of Scripture, and noticed that Genesis 15 was already marked. I read where Abram (before the name change) was told by God not to fear; he was promised a "reward (that would) be very great (verse 1)."

What I noticed was Abram's quick response to God's promise. I am guessing it was a foregone conclusion in Abram's mind that his great reward would include heirs (who knows, maybe the entire conversation was not recorded), as he said in verse 2: *"O Lord God, what will You give me, since I am childless, and the heir of my house is Eliezer of Damascus?"* Eliezer was a slave who was born within Abram's household. The practice in those days was that sons of slaves would become surrogate sons to their barren owners; an inheritance would be willed to them as adoptive sons. God responded immediately: *"This man will not be your heir; but one who will come forth from your own body; he shall be your heir (verse 3)."*

Because I know this story so well, I stopped reading to reflect on Abram's life journey from that moment forward. God decreed blessings, a "very great" reward. Abram looked at his life based on what he was accustomed to seeing - the inheritance is usually passed down to a slave of a barren family. God blew his mind with His response, since his wife Sarai was very old and past her childbearing years. He was also quite old himself.

What happened afterward really made me think: God did not provide the solution to the "puzzle" that He had originally presented to Abram until many years later. So what do you think he did in the meantime? He and his wife tried to figure out a solution on their own!!! Logically speaking, men can sire children all their lives, but women normally past childbearing age do NOT have children. So, Sarah offered her slave to bear a son to her husband so an heir for this great reward would be available. After all, God had said his great reward included a son from Abraham's own loins, correct? But didn't God already say that another slave (Eliezer) would not inherit this reward??? So why did they insist on creating a "legitimate" child with another slave??

God observed what they did to create a solution, by having Ishmael, and because of the binding covenant He had made with Abram earlier (his name was changed to Abraham by God), he still blessed Ishmael. Later, after Ishmael's birth, God spoke to Abraham again, saying that he would have another son. Abraham was amazed at God's words, so he presented Ishmael to God (see chapter 17 verse 18) by saying *"Oh that Ishmael might live before You!"* God responded immediately with these IMPOSSIBLE words: *"No, but Sarah (her name was changed by God as well) your wife will bear you a son, and you shall call his name Isaac; and I will establish My covenant with him for an everlasting covenant for his descendants after him (verse 19)."* NOW HE TELLS ME, Abraham was probably thinking to himself.

I want you to reflect on this: The covenant that God made between Himself and Abraham was binding, but it was only fully effective with individuals who were already in covenant with HIM!!! So Eliezer didn't get in on it, and Ishmael received only a portion, but Isaac, the son of Abraham's legitimate, COVENANT wife, would be the only one to benefit from this very great reward that God had promised!!!!

Those who are not in covenant with God, often try to fool themselves into believing that they will receive God's full benefits and His very great rewards! For example, if two people are living together outside of the covenant of marriage, the bed they sleep in is considered defiled by God - even if they

The Covenant

live their entire lives together, raise their children well and teach them to become responsible citizens in society. God still honors covenants, including the marriage covenant. It does not mean that people who choose to live outside of God's covenants won't live good lives nor receive blessings, but covenant people are the only ones who can FULLY benefit from God!

This floored me today. I had to do a self-check. Am I in covenant with God? Is my life up to par? Is my Christian walk worthy of Him looking my way and saying "Michelle, you will receive a very great reward from Me?"

When I arrived at the picnic, my mentor and friend said something to me that caused me to reflect on this topic again: "Focus just on your relationship with God; do not allow anybody else or anything else to get in the way of that as you will have to answer directly to Him about everything. Place Him as your main focus (and not on things you can get from Him - like a genie) and watch what He does! All your desires and needs will be met."

Isn't that what Abraham did in the beginning? He worshipped God, and left his family and friends behind to pursue God's promises to him. But notice that even he got weary of the long wait (between the Word and its manifestation), and took matters into his own hands. His "proactive" behavior reaped significant results, as both brothers are the patriarchs of today's Arabs and Jews.

My point: Let us stay focused, keep our eyes on God and review His precious promises to us regularly. If we stay the course and refrain from trying to find our own solutions for the blessings He promised, we will reap our great rewards with a heart filled with peace and joy. This is all just a test; God leaves out the details of the promises to see how much we are willing to trust Him completely. He is the One who decided to extend a covenant unto us; surely He knows exactly what needs to be done to fulfill that covenant! RELAX!!!! It's under His control.

| **It's My Life** *and I Live Here* |

"For My thoughts are not your thoughts, Nor are your ways My ways," declares the LORD. **(Isaiah 55:8, NASB)**

All Scriptural references were taken from the New American Standard Version, unless otherwise indicated.

Want to Marry? Let God Choose!

(Apr 2011)

Recently I have been pressing in with prayer on marriage. It is my desire to remarry and there are certain lessons I have learned recently. I would like to share them with you.

> **1. God is MOST concerned about spiritual compatibility AND purpose compatibility more than anything else.** *If we are unequally yoked with an unbeliever or with someone whose spiritual level is different from ours then we will not make it as a couple. This is regardless of income, community status, corporate status or church status. Our purpose MUST line up as well. What were we called to do? Who are we supposed to be? With the wrong spouse in our lives we may get to our purpose, but we may struggle a lot more to meet it. Or we may never do it at all. With the right person, things flow between both of you. There is an understanding and compatibility that resembles a glove that fits a hand well. Friction is at a minimum as you are both heading in the same direction. The tug-of-war feeling dissipates when the purpose of both marriage partners are aligned.*
>
> **2. Appearance and other temporal factors (such as skin tone, height, weight, earnings, education, etc.) matters more to us than it does to God.** *We sometimes miss God because of what we consider to be right for us. What if your perfect spouse is 5 inches taller than you and much darker than you would have preferred? What if he is a mechanic by day, but a student of the Word in the evenings because he is preparing to preach the gospel? What if she doesn't have long, flowing hair but she has creative ideas that can help you with your business? Many happily married people have stated that their spouses were right before their eyes, but until God unveiled their partner, they thought he or she was just another person (or just a good friend).*
>
> **3. God does NOT need our help in finding a spouse.** *He does, however, need our cooperation. We need to prepare ourselves to receive who He has tailor-made just for us. This also means that our biases (racial, educational, financial, appearance, etc.) must be laid out before Him so that He can work*

on us. We may decide it is time to search for a spouse, so we do what we've always done: We get hooked up on blind dates, or we scope out the church for a brother or a sister. What I am learning is that these things can help us meet new people, but we need to go to God DIRECTLY when seeking a spouse. Sometimes the person we think is right for us is not God's best. He knows what we need. He knows WHO we need. And He knows what we need for the future. Our vision is only for the present, but God knows our entire life story, and who would be best to help us fill in all the details and to share our experiences with us.

4. Our dependence on God for a spouse shows that we trust Him fully with our lives. When we insist on finding the love of our lives based on our qualifications, and present them to God (which is what I did the first time), things are disordered and we must be willing to handle the consequences. If we depend on God to select our mates, then He is held fully responsible for how things turn out. And trust me, if He has ANYTHING to do with it, the marriage will be a match made in Heaven! This does not mean disagreements won't come, nor does it mean sickness or financial trouble won't appear, but you will have such a strong foundation, that you will not be shaken by what comes. And divorce won't be on your mind, either.

Many of us surrendered our hearts to Jesus Christ to be Savior, but we will take a lifetime in allowing Him to become Lord over all aspects of our lives. Let us allow Him into this very important area, that of choosing a spouse for us.

Contact
Michelle G. Cameron

Website | www.michellegcameron.com

Email | info@michellegcameron.com

Facebook | https://www.facebook.com/MichelleGCameronLLC

Instagram | https://www.instagram.com/michellegcameronllc

Let's stay in touch!

www.ingramcontent.com/pod-product-compliance
Lightning Source LLC
Chambersburg PA
CBHW051453290426
44109CB00016B/1734